THE FICTIONAL TECHNIQUE
OF
SCOTT FITZGERALD

INTERNATIONAL SCHOLARS FORUM

A SERIES OF BOOKS BY AMERICAN SCHOLARS

9

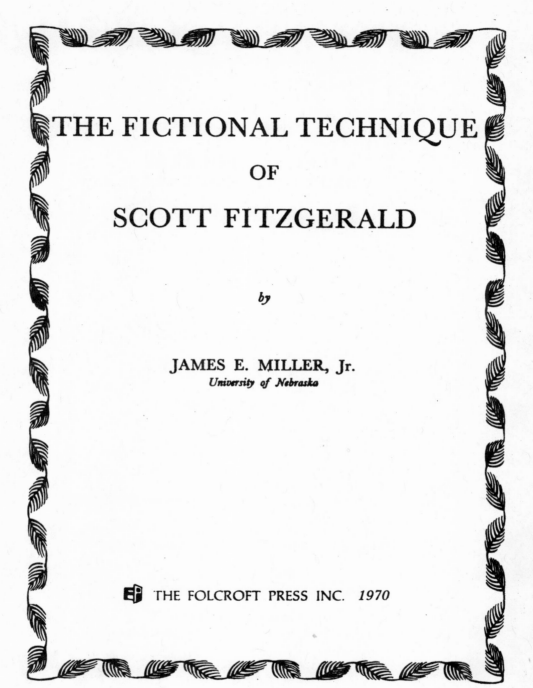

THE FICTIONAL TECHNIQUE

OF

SCOTT FITZGERALD

by

JAMES E. MILLER, Jr.
University of Nebraska

THE FOLCROFT PRESS INC. *1970*

Limited to 150 Copies

THE FICTIONAL TECHNIQUE

OF

SCOTT FITZGERALD

by

JAMES E. MILLER, Jr.
University of Nebraska

THE HAGUE
MARTINUS NIJHOFF
1957

FOR BARBARA

PREFACE

In 1925 T. S. Eliot wrote to F. Scott Fitzgerald that he had read *The Great Gatsby* three times and that it had "excited" him more than any new novel, English or American, for a number of years. He added: "When I have time I should like to write to you more fully and tell you exactly why it seems to me such a remarkable book. In fact it seems to me to be the first step that American fiction has taken since Henry James."[1] Unfortunately Mr. Eliot has failed to amplify and explain his statement, but it would seem safe to assume that he was referring to the *technique* in *The Great Gatsby*, especially since Henry James's major contribution to fiction is considered to be primarily in the realm of technique. In any case, most critics have agreed that *The Great Gatsby* is an important achievement in technique. Only five years separate *The Great Gatsby* from *This Side of Paradise*, Fitzgerald's first novel, but these novels are much further apart in technique than this brief period would lead one to expect. *This Side of Paradise* represents one tradition in literature which stands directly opposed to the tradition which *The Great Gatsby* represents. This opposition was brought to dramatic focus by the intricate James-Wells controversy, which culminated in an exchange of letters in July, 1915 – five years before Fitzgerald's first book appeared. Fitzgerald's shift from the use of one kind of technique to its opposite and the causes for that shift must command the primary attention in any examination of Fitzgerald's development as a novelist. In this study, main consideration has been given to the technique of *This Side of Paradise* (1920), *The Beautiful and Damned* (1922), and *The Great Gatsby* (1925), as these are Fitzgerald's major works during the crucial period of his transition. Fitzgerald's short fiction of this period has also been examined, however, whenever it has illuminated his technique in the novel.

The term "technique," like most critical terms, has had different meanings for different novelists and critics. It is almost impossible to speak of technique in modern fiction without referring to three novelists: Henry James, Joseph Conrad, and James Joyce. As one critic has said: "Under the 'immense artistic preoccupations' of James and Conrad and Joyce, the form of the novel changed, and with the technical

---

[1] T. S. Eliot, one of "Three Letters About *The Great Gatsby*," *The Crack-Up*, ed. by Edmund Wilson (New York: James Laughlin for New Directions, 1945), p. 310.

change, analogous changes took place in substance, in point of view, in the whole conception of fiction."[2] It is from these three writers that most of the recent theorists on technique in fiction have taken their cue. In 1921, Percy Lubbock published *The Craft of Fiction*, something of a landmark in the criticism of fictional technique. But his was a somewhat limited view of the term: "The whole intricate question of method, in the craft of fiction, I take to be governed by the question of the point of view – the question of the relation in which the narrator stands to the story."[3] Joseph Warren Beach, in *The Twentieth Century Novel: Studies in Technique* (1932), does not attempt a comprehensive definition of technique but simply calls it "the way the story is... told" or "the means by which" the author realizes his "intentions."[4] Mark Schorer, in a recent essay entitled "Technique as Discovery," extends the definition of technique much further than his predecessors: it is, he says, the "arrangement of events to create plot," and, within plot, "suspense, and climax"; it is the "means of revealing character motivation, relationship and development"; it is the use of point of view, not only to "heighten dramatic interest through the narrowing or broadening of perspective upon the material," but also "as a means toward the positive definition of theme"; it is, finally, the use of language "to create a certain texture and tone which in themselves state and define themes and meanings." In this definition, "technique" encompasses almost the whole of the novel: "Everything is technique which is not the lump of experience itself, and one cannot properly say that a writer has no technique, or that he eschews technique, for, being a writer, he cannot do so."[5] It is in this comprehensive sense that the term has been used in this study. Of course, certain limitations, not of definition but of purpose, have been necessary. Insofar as it has been possible, the study has centered consideration on three elements of technique: the development of theme, point of view, and the manner of representing events. Other matters of technique, when they have illuminated these or when they have appeared vital in themselves, have also received attention.

---

[2] Mark Schorer, "Technique as Discovery," *Forms of Modern Fiction*, ed. by William Van O'Connor (Minneapolis: The University of Minnesota Press, 1948), p. 16.
[3] Percy Lubbock, *The Craft of Fiction* (New York: Peter Smith, 1921), p. 251.
[4] Joseph Warren Beach, *The Twentieth Century Novel: Studies in Technique* (New York: Appleton-Century-Crofts, Inc., 1932), pp. 3-4.
[5] Schorer, "Technique as Discovery," *op. cit.*, pp. 10-11.

For what they taught me about the study of literature, I express my thanks to Professors Walter Blair, Napier Wilt, and Morton D. Zabel of the University of Chicago. Their assistance has been exceeded only by their encouragement: for both I am grateful. Any student of F. Scott Fitzgerald must owe much to the novelist's biographer, Arthur Mizener. His courtesies to me have been many and generous. Although my debt to these and other scholars and critics is great, responsibility for the judgments or misjudgments of this book is solely mine.

For permission to quote from F. Scott Fitzgerald's *This Side of Paradise, Flappers and Philosophers, The Beautiful and Damned, Tales of the Jazz Age, The Vegetable, The Great Gatsby, All the Sad Young Men, Tender Is the Night, Taps at Reveille,* and *The Last Tycoon,* I am deeply grateful to the publisher, Charles Scribner's Sons. For permission to quote from Fitzgerald's *The Crack-Up,* I am indebted to the publisher, New Directions. Special permission has been granted by a number of publishers to quote from a number of other books: Joseph Warren Beach, *The Twentieth Century Novel: Studies in Technique,* published by Appleton-Century-Crofts, Inc.; Charles C. Baldwin, *The Men Who Make Our Novels,* published by Dodd, Mead & Company; Alfred Kazin, *On Native Grounds,* published by Harcourt, Brace and Company, Inc.; Robert Hugh Benson, *None Other Gods,* published by B. Herder Book Company; Arthur Mizener, *The Far Side of Paradise,* Willa Cather, *My Ántonia,* and Maxwell Geismar, *The Last of the Provincials: the American Novel, 1915–1925,* all published by Houghton Mifflin Company; H. L. Mencken, *Prejudices: Second Series* and Willa Cather, *A Lost Lady,* both published by Alfred A. Knopf; Oscar Cargill, *Intellectual America: Ideas on the March,* published by The Macmillan Company; Harlan Hatcher, *Creating the Modern American Novel,* published by Rinehart and Company; Henry James, *Notes on Novelists* and *The Art of the Novel,* and Percy Lubbock, *The Craft of Fiction,* all published by Charles Scribner's Sons; John O'Hara, "Introduction" to *The Portable F. Scott Fitzgerald,* published by The Viking Press, Inc.

CONTENTS

★

Preface VII
Acknowledgments IX

THIS SIDE OF PARADISE

A NOVEL OF SATURATION 1
Wells and James: Saturation vs. Selection 2
This Side of Paradise as Quest Book 13
A Gesture of Indefinite Revolt 20

THE BEAUTIFUL AND DAMNED

A NOVEL OF TRANSITION
From Mackenzie to Mencken 39
Flappers, Philosophers, and the Jazz Age 43
The Meaninglessness of Life 51

THE GREAT GATSBY

A NOVEL OF SELECTION
The Art of Magic Suggestiveness 67
Those Sad Young Men: A Moving Experience 81
Boats Against the Current 89
Without This – Nothing 108

CONCLUSION 115

1: *THIS SIDE OF PARADISE*

A NOVEL OF SATURATION

F. Scott Fitzgerald has left neither an essay on critical theory nor any significant amount of criticism from which his literary theories may be ascertained. Some critics, impressed by this lack and by the great amount of mediocre fiction which Fitzgerald turned out for the popular magazines, have assumed that the undeniable artistry of *The Great Gatsby* was some kind of accident, produced by a "natural" (or instinctive) but erratic talent. Fitzgerald's biographer, Arthur Mizener, stressed what he called Fitzgerald's "intuitive way of working."[1] One critic, noting that *The Great Gatsby* was "out of line" with Fitzgerald's other fiction, concluded that it was "important for the author's reputation to know that it was consciously different and not merely accidentally so."[2] Although the premise of this statement is doubtful in itself, it can be shown that Fitzgerald was far more conscious of what he was doing in his work than is commonly supposed. But as a basis for exploring Fitzgerald's literary consciousness, it is useful first to relate him to one of the most significant literary events of his time. True, that event has become important (and indeed known) only in retrospect, because a number of the crucial documents in the event have come to light only after it has passed into history; but most historians of contemporary literature have found the event a dramatization, in concrete terms, of the clash of two opposing forces or movements in our literature. The event is the James-Wells controversy which reached its climax and conclusion in the exchange of personal letters in July, 1915.

Fitzgerald did not participate in this controversy, and, indeed, he may not even have been aware that it was in progress. But when he began his literary career with *This Side of Paradise*, he was under the influence of the literary movement to which Wells was wholeheartedly dedicated; and in the next few years, he gradually became aware of the opposing movement which was vigorously supported by James. By the time he wrote *The Great Gatsby* Fitzgerald had completely shifted his allegiance. Evidence exists to show that Fitzgerald was familiar with some of the documents of the Wells-James debate and with many of the writers who were the focus of the controversy. As a writer matur-

[1] Arthur Mizener, *The Far Side of Paradise* (Boston: Houghton Mifflin Company, 1951), p. 170.

[2] Oscar Cargill, *Intellectual America: Ideas on the March* (New York: The Macmillan Company, 1941), p. 344.

ing in the midst of these opposing literary forces and moving from one side to the other, Fitzgerald serves dramatically to exhibit the significant impact on novelists of these clashing movements in literary theory. Just as James and Wells propound the theories, Fitzgerald serves as the example – all the more interesting in that he is the example for both sides. Moreover, Fitzgerald's movement away from one tradition and toward another exemplifies the general trend in the literature of America during the contemporary period. In order to understand Fitzgerald's development in fictional technique, it is important at the beginning to view him in his literary context; this context can best be brought to focus by an examination of the Wells-James debate.

I. WELLS AND JAMES: SATURATION VS. SELECTION

Before James and Wells attacked each other as symbols of what they disliked most in the novel, they wrote essays on the novel of their time in which they agreed only in what they saw – the domination of the "loosely-constructed" novel. Wells was delighted with what he discovered; James was disturbed. Wells, in his essay called "The Contemporary Novel" (1911), approved of the growing popularity of the loosely-constructed, discursive type of novel. He granted that the short story should aim at producing "one single, vivid effect," but the novel, he believed, was different: "the novel I hold to be a discursive thing; it is not a single interest, but a woven tapestry of interests; one is drawn on first by this affection and curiosity and then by that."[3]

In this early essay, Wells came to at least four distinct conclusions, all of which are importantly related to technique. He thought that character, rather than action, should be the center of the novel: "The distinctive value of the novel among written works of art is in characterization, and the charm of a well-conceived character lies, not in knowing its destiny, but in watching its proceedings."[4] It easily follows that if happenings or events are valued in relation to character rather than in relation to action or plot, a somewhat loose basis for *relevance* is applicable. And Wells's next point was concerned with relevance. He was disturbed, he said, at the reviews of novels which complained that "this, that, or the other thing in a novel is irrelevant,"; "nothing," he said, "is irrelevant if the writer's mood is happy."[5] Perhaps Wells

[3] H. G. Wells, "The Contemporary Novel," *Fortnightly Review*, XCVI (November, 1911), 862–63.
[4] *Ibid.*, p. 863.
[5] *Ibid.*, p. 864.

meant that a novel derived its unity not from a self-contained plot or theme but from the author's pervading feeling or "mood," but his point is vaguely put. In any case, he reduced the test of *relevance* to an almost negligible position for the writer and critic.

It is not surprising, in view of the "discursive" type of novel for which Wells was pleading, that he should make a special defense for the intrusion of the author. He must have seen, as did Joseph Warren Beach later, ("In a bird's eye view of the English novel from Fielding to Ford, the one thing that will impress you more than any other is the disappearance of the author"),[6] that, in the modern development of the novel, the author was effacing himself, attempting to disappear, as an external commentator on the story, completely. His argument for the intruding author was, logically enough, a historical one: "Nearly all of the novels that have, by the lapse of time, reached an assured position of recognized greatness, are not only saturated in the personality of the author, but have, in addition, quite unaffected personal outbreaks." Author-intervention, he thought, when done without affectation, "gives a sort of depth, a sort of subjective reality, that no such cold, almost affectedly ironical detachment... can ever attain."[7] Perhaps the main reason that Wells argued for the right of the author to step forth in a novel in his own person was that he looked upon the novel as fulfilling a special purpose. "So far as I can see," he said, "the novel is the only medium through which we can discuss the great majority of the problems which are being raised in such bristling multitude by our contemporary social development."[8] It is much easier, of course, for the novelist to indicate his approval or disapproval, his likes or dislikes, by simply stepping forth in his own right rather than by remaining concealed and letting his art or craftsmanship do the work for him. Wells's view of the purpose of the novel was not modest: "You see now the scope of the claim I am making for the novel; it is to be the social mediator, the vehicle of understanding, the instrument of self-examination, the parade of morals and the exchange of manners, the factory of customs, the criticism of laws and institutions and of social dogmas and ideas.... Before we have done, we will have all life within the scope of the novel."[9] One function of the novel seems to have escaped Wells entirely – its function as a work of art designed to evoke certain emotional responses.

[6] Joseph Warren Beach, *op. cit.*, p. 14.
[7] Wells, "The Contemporary Novel," *op. cit.*, pp. 864–65.
[8] *Ibid.*, p. 869.
[9] *Ibid.*, pp. 872–73.

These four concepts (character as the center of the novel, very little or nothing as irrelevant in the novel, author-intrusion as a virtue in the novel, and the novel as a vehicle for problem-discussion) can probably be best implied by Wells's term "discursive." Since they are directly concerned with technique, and since, as Wells saw, they constituted a movement which, at the time he wrote, was dominating literature, Wells's statement of them is actually a statement of an important historical influence bound to affect writers of his era in matters of technique. It was not, of course, necessary for these writers to be familiar with Wells's theories or generalizations: they had only to know and be influenced by his novels and the novels of his "school," the practical results of the theory.

If Wells in 1911 looked happily upon the ascendancy of the discursive novel, in 1914 James frowned upon its holding the field. Wells's essay was in a way a defense, implying an opposition. James was probably the best qualified novelist of the time to present the case for the opposition. His essay, "The New Novel" (1914), represents the voice of a "movement" which, as Wells asserted and James admitted, was, as an influence, much the weaker of the two. Adherents to it were few and its spokesmen even fewer. But Wells had thought this influence significant enough to write *against*, and to James it was vital enough to defend vigorously. Surveying the literary scene in 1914, James saw H. G. Wells, Arnold Bennett, D. H. Lawrence, Gilbert Cannan, Compton Mackenzie, and Hugh Walpole as having "gathered themselves up with a movement never yet undertaken on our literary scene." After noting the "sharpest differences of character and range" in the authors, James said that "they yet come together under our so convenient measure of value by *saturation*." James, as usual, left the term "saturation" to imply in itself much of its meaning, but one can see readily its relation to Wells's term, "discursive." "To be saturated," said James, "is to be documented, to be able even on occasion to prove quite enviably and potently so." But it was not of mere documentation that James spoke; there was a passion or energy motivating the writing: "The act of squeezing out to the utmost the plump and more or less juicy orange of a particular acquainted state and letting this affirmation of energy, however directed or undirected, constitute for them the 'treatment' of a theme – that is what we remark them as mainly engaged in, after remarking the example so strikingly, so originally set, even if an undue subjection to it be here and there repudiated."[10] This "affirmation of

[10] Henry James, "The New Novel," *Notes on Novelists* (New York: Charles Scribner's Sons, 1916), pp. 319–25.

energy" recalls Wells's statement that "nothing is irrelevant if the writer's mood is happy." One sees readily that the question of *relevance* was for James the prime question.

Having noted and defined the movement for which we have seen Wells as spokesman, James hastened to point out what he saw of value in it. "Nothing is further from our thought than to undervalue saturation and possession, the fact of the particular experience, the state and degree of acquaintance incurred, however such a consciousness may have been determined." But, continued James, "these things represent on the part of the novelist... just one half of his authority – the other half being represented of course by the application he is inspired to make of them."[11] By "the other half," James meant the application of art to the experiences of life to produce a particular piece of fiction. He spoke of the "last true touch," by which he meant "the touch of the hand of selection." He asserted that "the principle of selection has been involved at the worst or the least... in any approach whatever to the loaf of life." For, after all, "there being no question of a slice upon which the further question of where and how to cut it does not wait, the office of method, the idea of choice and comparison, have occupied the ground from the first." James thus proposed "selection" as the preferred alternative to "saturation," the extract from life as a substitute for the slice of life. And, as he pointed out, the choice is really not so much of a choice after all. There must be selection even in saturation, there must be a way and method of cutting even the slice of life ("there can be no such thing as an amorphous slice"); the novelist has only the choice either of recognising this inevitability, and consciously making decisions as to method, or of ignoring this obligation, and cutting the slice blindly.[12] If he chooses the former course, the novelist must have a "centre of interest," a "controlling idea," or a "pointed intention." Too much emphasis cannot, for James, be placed on *centre*, *controlling*, and *pointed*, for, before the novelist can intelligently make decisions concerning the method of *embodying* his intention, he must have his specific intention firmly in mind.

In the latter part of his essay, James tested his "theories" by applying them to specific cases. Two of those whom he classified as novelists of saturation, H. G. Wells and Compton Mackenzie, have most interest in a study of Fitzgerald's technique, for they were Fitzgerald's literary idols at the time he started his career as a novelist. Of special interest are James's references to *Sinister Street*, since it (as will be seen) was the

[11] *Ibid.*, p. 326.
[12] *Ibid.* p. 342.

direct model for Fitzgerald's first novel, *This Side of Paradise*. James remarked of *Sinister Street*, "If a boy's experience has ever been given us for its face value simply, for what it is worth in mere recovered intensity, it is so given us here." Of all the saturation novels, "it can... scarce have helped being the most sufficient in itself." It is, said James, "from beginning to end the remembered and reported thing, that thing alone, that thing existent in the field of memory." But James admitted that *Sinister Street* gained value from "the applied intelligence... the lively talent, of the memoriser. The memoriser helps, he contributes, he completes." James posed what was for him the crucial critical question: what *Sinister Street* "may mean as a whole." He attempted to discover a controlling idea or a pointed intention or a center of interest – and failed: "In spite of our sense of being brushed from the first by a hundred subordinate purposes, the succession and alternation of which seem to make after a fashion a plan," – the purposes "fail to gather themselves for application or to converge to an idea."[13]

The two novelists whom James set over against the "saturationists" are Edith Wharton and Joseph Conrad, both of particular interest because Fitzgerald was later to be influenced by their work. Especially is Conrad of significance, for he stands in relation to *The Great Gatsby* much as Compton Mackenzie stands in relation to *This Side of Paradise*. In his discussion of *The Custom of the Country*, James said of Edith Wharton: "If... she too has clearly a saturation... we have it from her not in the crude state but in the extract, the extract that makes all the difference for our sense of an artistic economy." But James pointed to Conrad as the "supreme specimen of the part playable in a novel by the source of interest, the principle of provision attended to, for which we claim importance." James referred specifically to Conrad's *Chance*, which, he said, is "a signal instance of provision the most earnest and the most copious for its leaving ever so much to be said about the particular provision effected." The method of *Chance*, thought James, represented an innovation in technique: "[*Chance*] is none the less an extraordinary exhibition of method by the fact that the method is, we venture to say, without precedent in any like work."[14]

The new method which James attributed to Conrad was the "multiplying [of] his creators or, as we are now fond of saying, producers, as to make them almost more numerous and quite emphatically more material than the creatures and the production itself in whom and which we by the general law of fiction expect such agents to lose

[13] *Ibid.*, pp. 357–61.
[14] *Ibid.*, pp. 345–54.

themselves." This "general law of fiction" is directly opposed to the author-intervention for which Wells had pleaded. James asserted, "We take for granted by the general law of fiction a primary author, take him so much for granted that we forget him in proportion as he works upon us, and that he works upon us most in fact by making us forget him."[15] In other words, James believed that that author is best who is heard but not seen, that that method is best which succeeds without obtruding, that that art is best which is not apparent as art. This "law" precludes the author's stepping forward to chat with the reader. Conrad had developed his narrator or narrators as characters within the framework of his story, a technique far different from the author-intrusion so precious to Wells.

Wells's reaction to James's "The New Novel" was set forth in an odd book called *Boon, The Mind of the Race, The Wild Asses of the Devil, and The Last Trump* (1915). Wells remarked of the book (*Notes on Novelists*) in which James's essay had appeared: "It's one sustained demand for the picture effect. Which is a denial of the sweet complexity of life…. The picture… is forced to a unity because it can see only one aspect at a time." Wells reiterated the arguments which he first presented in "The Contemporary Novel." The novel "must be various and discursive," he said, if it is to follow life. For "life is diversity and entertainment, not completeness and satisfaction. All actions are halfhearted, shot delightfully with wandering thoughts – about something else. All true stories are a felt of irrelevancies." Wells continued to see the novel as some kind of literal transcription of life. James's plea for method or selection, which would give the illusion or effect of the complexity of life without in itself being discursive and irrelevant, seems to have eluded Wells's comprehension entirely. James, said Wells, "talks of 'selection,' and of making all of a novel definitely *about* a theme. He objects to a 'saturation' that isn't oriented. And he objects, if you go into it, for no clear reason at all."[16] It is surprising how much of James Wells comprehended and how much, in the real sense, he didn't understand at all.

But Wells left the realm of theory and got down to a specific case – the case of James's novels. Wells said that he objected to them because "James sets out to make… [them] with the presupposition that they can be made continuously relevant." James would certainly have had no objection to this statement. But Wells followed the assertion with a

---

[15] *Ibid.*, p. 347.
[16] H. G. Wells. *Boon, The Mind of the Race, The Wild Asses of the Devil, and The Last Trump* (New York: George H. Doran Company, 1915), pp. 105–07.

grave charge – grave, at least, in James's eyes. Follow up, said Wells, James's conception of selection as it affects his own works: "In practice James's selection becomes just omission and nothing more. He omits everything that demands digressive treatment or collateral statement."[17] Although it is not the purpose here to make a study of James's novels in order to test Wells's charge, it can readily be shown that James's conception of selection was not merely omission. And since "selection" was a key term for James, perhaps Wells's charge was the crucial point of the debate. In his prefaces to the 1907 New York edition of his work, James spoke of "the successfully foreshortened thing, where representation is arrived at... not by the addition of items... but by the art of figuring synthetically, a compactness into which the imagination may cut thick, as into the rich density of a wedding-cake."[18] Selection (or foreshortening) was for James, a matter of technique rather than of quantity; selection was not mere addition nor omission, but a "figuring synthetically" or a *method* of treatment. Wells desired irrelevance in order to imitate life; James desired selection in order to convey the *effect* of life.

In the Wells-James debate, the first intense concern for theory was followed by an increasing amount of personal reference, which exploded at last in Wells' direct attack on James' novels. Rarely have opposing literary ideas come to blows so fully in public view. For up to the publication of Wells' *Boon* the controversy had been public. But from this point on, the two antagonists retreated from the public's eye and carried on the battle by personal correspondence. In a letter to Wells, James objected to the rough treatment which he had received in *Boon*. But James's position was, as it had been from the beginning, conciliatory: "The fine thing about the fictional form to me is that it opens such widely different windows of attention; but that is just why I like the window so to frame the play and the process."[19] At first James seemed to be saying that he and Wells differed in their conceptions of the novel and that it was simply a matter of taste as to which was preferred. But ingeniously using the figure of the window, James suggested the absolute necessity of the frame – that is, selection. There can be no window without a frame, and if there is no window, then the novelist is lost in the great mass of amorphous life itself.

Wells answered James with abject apologies for having offended him.

[17] *Ibid.*, pp. 106–07.
[18] James, *The Art of the Novel: Critical Prefaces* (New York: Charles Scribner's Sons, 1947), pp. 87–88.
[19] Henry James, *Letters*, ed. by Percy Lubbock (London: Macmillan and Co., Ltd., 1920), II, 505.

Boon, he said, was "just a waste-paper basket" of literary remains found in his desk. And he startlingly asserted, "I had rather be called a journalist than an artist, that is the essence of it, and there was no other antagonist possible than yourself." James answered Wells's figure of the wastebasket by simply extending it: "Your comparison of the book to a waste-basket strikes me as the reverse of felicitous, for what one throws into that receptacle is exactly what one doesn't commit to publicity and make the affirmation of one's estimate of one's contemporaries by." And James' last say was, appropriately, on art: "It is art that *makes* life, makes interest, makes importance, for our consideration and application of these things, and I know of no substitute whatever for the force and beauty of its process." James knew that the controversy, to be a controversy at all, had to begin and end with art as the center. The question for him was simply the nature of the artistry. Wells's reply ("I don't clearly understand your concluding phrases – which shows no doubt how completely they define our difference") shows how completely different were the points from which they started and how far off was a meeting of their minds.[20]

Wells put his finger on the causes of the "fundamental difference" between himself and James when he said, "To you literature like painting is an end, to me literature like architecture is a means, it has a use." James answered that "there is no sense in which architecture is aesthetically 'for use' that doesn't leave any other art whatever as much so."[21] Wells, however, was not referring to the "aesthetic" use of architecture, but rather to its more practical use. To James, the novel was a work of art; to Wells it was a vehicle – a vehicle for the discussion of social and other problems. Out of this fundamental difference grew the many other differences. James's words, "saturation" and "selection," are excellent terms for suggesting these differences. In the novel of saturation, irrelevance is a virtue because it makes the novel more lifelike; it lends credibility to the "slice of life." In the novel of selection, relevance is a virtue, because it emphasizes the "pointed intention" or "centre of interest." The manner and method of selection are of prime importance and give rise to the question as to how the story is to be told. These differences underlie another difference. In the novel of saturation, the novelist, to achieve "depth" and "subjective reality," may step forth and speak in his own voice; in the novel of selection, the novelist cannot intrude without violating the "general law of fiction."

Although the Wells-James debate had been carried on in England,

[20] *Ibid.*, pp. 505–508.
[21] *Ibid.*

the two opposed forces represented by it made themselves felt on the literary scene in the United States during the crucial period of Fitzgerald's artistic development, 1920 to 1925. At the beginning of this period had appeared the so-called "new" literature. Archibald Marshall, a British novelist, was given a group of new novels to review in 1921 which were "said to represent a new development in American fiction." Among the novels were *Main Street* by Sinclair Lewis, *Moon-Calf* by Floyd Dell, *Poor White* by Sherwood Anderson, and *Miss Lulu Bett* by Zona Gale. The adverse criticism made by Marshall tended in one direction. Of *Main Street* he said, "The weakness of [Sinclair Lewis's] book is that it doesn't make a story, but only creates an atmosphere." *Moon-Calf* he found to be "a series of apparently unrelated episodes, with no deeper meaning to them... than what appeared on the surface." From these few remarks it might appear that the "new" development in American literature after World War I was simply a variation of the saturation novel, with its lack of a pointed intention, with its irrelevance, with its piling up detail on detail. But Archibald Marshall saw some encouraging signs. *Poor White* was, he thought, "fine and direct," and *Miss Lulu Bett* showed "an admirable artistic restraint." The reviewer noted that, although the novel was "a good deal less than half the length" of the others, it did all that they did and more.[22] In this English critic's view, the "new" realism, although predominantly *saturation*, had some *selection* in it; it was capable of being embodied in either "form."

In April, 1922, a supplement to *The New Republic* called "The Novel of Tomorrow and the Scope of Fiction" appeared. Contributors to this issue were Mary Austin, James Branch Cabell, Willa Cather, Floyd Dell, Theodore Dreiser, Waldo Frank, Zona Gale, Joseph Hergesheimer, Robert Herrick, William Allen White, and others. In a series of essays these writers presented their theories of the novel, all starting, more or less, from the same point of departure. Apparently *The New Republic* had sent to each of them, in order to indicate appropriate subject matter, the title it planned to use for the supplement. This collection of essays represents a rare thing in literary history – a summary of most of the conflicting theories of an art-form expressed at a single moment in time by the leading artists themselves. This "symposium" is extremely useful in isolating and examining the trends or movements which influenced Fitzgerald's concept of the novel.

The problem with which all of the writers were confronted was that

[22] Archibald Marshall, "A Browse Among the Best Sellers." *The Bookman*, LIV (September, 1921), 8–12.

expressed by Mary Austin: "American novelists are often accused of a failure of form." There were three possible lines of approach to the problem. The lack of form could be defended; it could be brushed aside as of little importance; and it could be attacked. Mary Austin believed that the accusation of a failure of form was nothing "more than an admission of failure of access on the part of the critics." She believed that the "democratic novelist must be inside his novel rather than outside."[23] Theodore Dreiser, in his essay entitled "The Scope of Fiction," said that "the problem of scope must ever be personal and individual. It is not for academic interpretation or fixation."[24] Dreiser, like Wells, would leave the matter of relevance to the taste, or "mood," of the author. Neither of them, apparently, recognized the existence of any criteria of form external to the author.

Floyd Dell, writing of "The Difference Between Life and Fiction," took a middle course. He admitted that life "in the raw" needed simplification, that there must be a "suppressing, altering, rearranging [of] the facts, [to] permit what is left to have some emotional meaning." But, he pointed out, "No one... who has any very acute sense of the variety and jumbled irrelevance of the facts of life... would either imagine that the literal record of these facts constituted a story, or be so ambitious as to attempt to frame them *all* into an intelligible emotional sequence."[25] There is some kind of selection in every novelist, even, as Dell said, in Theodore Dreiser. What Floyd Dell seems to imply is that, since every novelist does select, he has some kind of form; therefore, the question of form is not an important one, and perhaps not really a question at all.

Probably the most significant article in this symposium in suggesting the current literary trends was the opening essay, Phil'p Littell's review of Percy Lubbock's *The Craft of Fiction*. That a discussion of such a book, which is concerned so acutely with the importance of technique in fiction, should stand at the beginning of the discussion indicates in itself the growing concern of American novelists for form and method. Mr. Littell concluded his review by remarking of Percy Lubbock: "He could teach our youngest novelists what questions to ask themselves before setting to work."[26] These questions would, of course, be about technique – particularly about point of view. And it would not be long before most of the young novelists would be asking themselves just

[23] Mary Austin, "The American Form of the Novel," *The New Republic*, XXX (April 12, 1922), 4.
[24] Theodore Dreiser, "The Scope of Fiction," *ibid.*, p. 9.
[25] Floyd Dell, "The Difference Between Life and Fiction," *ibid.*, p. 7.
[26] Philip Littell, "The Craft of Fiction," *ibid.*, p. 2.

such questions. Zona Gale indicated as much in her essay, "The Novel of Tomorrow." She saw, in the development of the modern novel, "a form suitable for the expression of reality." This form was "direct, unreflective, highly selective... in immediate contact with its material ... uncompromising, tactless, unashamed." The style was "bare and clear as a plain."[27] This view of the novel was close to Henry James's concept as embodied in his term *selection*.

But it was left to Willa Cather (who figured importantly in Fitzgerald's development), in "The Novel Démeublé," to state the case for selection most clearly, and to point the direction for the novel to take. She saw the issue much as did James when she said, "If the novel is a form of imaginative art, it cannot be at the same time a vivid and brilliant form of journalism." And it was the trend toward selection that she noted when she remarked: "There are hopeful signs that some of the younger writers are trying to break away from mere verisimilitude, and, following the development of modern painting, to interpret imaginatively the material and social investiture of their characters; to present their scene by suggestion rather than by enumeration." The novel, thought Miss Cather, could progress only toward selection if it would "develop into anything more varied and perfect than all the many novels that have gone before." To present a scene "by suggestion" is similar to James's "figuring synthetically." Willa Cather understood, as did James, that selection was not mere omission: "Whatever is felt upon the page without being specifically named there – that, one might say, is created." Thus the fact or experience that is selected suggests much more than it in itself is. It symbolizes – it creates: "It is the inexplicable presence of the thing not named, of the overtone divined by the ear but not heard by it, the verbal mood, the emotional aura of the fact or the thing or the deed, that gives high quality to the novel." Emotions, thought Willa Cather, were "killed by tasteless amplitude." And she concluded: "How wonderful it would be if we could throw all the furniture out of the window; and along with it, all the meaningless reiterations."[28]

As this collection of essays shows, the views held by Wells and James were being debated on Fitzgerald's native grounds during his formative years as a novelist. And the trend was away from documentation or saturation toward selection and experimentation in technique. Although it would be difficult to assert the exact causes of this trend, such literary events as the appearance of Percy Lubbock's book on technique

[27] Zona Gale, ,"The Novel of Tomorrow," *ibid.*, p. 12.
[28] Willa Cather, "The Novel Démeublé," *ibid.*, p. 6.

in 1921 and the publication of James Joyce's *Ulysses* in 1922 undoubtedly figured importantly. New young critics such as Edmund Wilson
also played a part.[29] Later in the decade appeared the novels of Ernest
Hemingway, which tended toward the extreme in drama and thereby
left much to inference, or created much that was not explicitly stated;
there appeared also William Faulkner's novels, which were experimen-
tations in the new techniques. These novelists may by looked upon in
part as the effect of this trend toward selection and in part as the cause,
in the wide influence of their work. The trend developed eventually
into what might well be called the climax of it: the recent revival of
Henry James. James, standing both at the beginning and at the end,
dominated the entire movement. Joseph Warren Beach could say in
1942, in his *American Fiction: 1920–1940*: "Each one of the men I have
chosen to discuss has a marked and individual accent, giving esthetic
definition to all his offering, and that precious air of being selective."[30]
A historian of American literature of the period between the wars has
asserted: "If a trend in the handling of detail is to be discovered in the
interwar period, it is a trend toward selectivity and poetic suggestion
rather than exhaustive documentation."[31] Fitzgerald was not isolated,
then, in the development which is to be traced in his novels. The two
opposed views or attitudes, stated and defended by James and Wells,
were a part of the literary scene of Fitzgerald's place and time. Writers
were at hand to defend or exemplify the one or the other. In the main,
these opposed concepts of the novel centered around method or technique – the "how" of telling a story. Almost inevitably a young writer
was influenced by one of the two forces. It remains to be seen how these
influences, which constitute Fitzgerald's literary background, worked
on him and how they affected his novels.

II. 'THIS SIDE OF PARADISE' AS QUEST BOOK

Fitzgerald began the first version of *This Side of Paradise* during his
undergraduate days at Princeton. From the time that he started writing

[29] Edmund Wilson, in an article published in 1922 called "The Rag-Bag of the
Soul" (*The Literary Review of the New York Evening Post*, November 25, 1922, p. 238),
attempted to describe "the type towards which modern expression seems to *tend*."
He devoted much of his article to showing that "all the works [which form the type
he was describing] ... do not ... completely lack structure." He was particularly
interested in pointing out the "precise technical plan" of *Ulysses*.
[30] Joseph Warren Beach, *American Fiction: 1920–1940* (New York: The Macmillan
Company, 1942), p. 8.
[31] Walter Blair, Theodore Hornberger, and Randall Stewart, *The Literature of the
United States* (Chicago: Scott Foresman and Co., 1947), II, 870.

the novel up to the completion and publication of the third and final
version in 1920, Fitzgerald was, as his letters show, steeped in the
literature of the Wells side of the Wells-James controversy. His two
greatest literary enthusiasms were Wells and Compton Mackenzie. In
1917, he wrote to Edmund Wilson of a Wells novel: "I think that *The
New Machiavelli* is the greatest English novel of the century."[32] But
Fitzgerald's interest in Wells was not confined to his novels. In another
letter, he asked Wilson: "Have you read Well's [sic] *Boon, The Mind of
the Race*, (Doran – 1916) It's marvellous!"[33] *Boon*, as has been noted,
was one of the important documents in the Wells-James controversy;
it was an attack on the novel of selection, a defense of the novel of
saturation. Fitzgerald's approval cannot, of course, be taken as his
complete acceptance of all that Wells said in *Boon* – but his enthusiastic
remark is highly suggestive of his general attitude toward the novel.
In this same letter, Fitzgerald said, "I'm rather bored here [Princeton]
but I... read Wells and Rousseau. I read Mrs. Gerould's *British Novelists Limited* and think she underestimates Wells but is right in putting
McKenzie [sic] at the head of his school."[34] Fitzgerald remarked further
that he had reminded himself lately of, among others, "Michael Fane,
Maurice Avery & Guy Hazelwood," all of whom are characters in
Compton Mackenzie's early novels. It is highly revealing that Fitzgerald, at the time of writing *This Side of Paradise*, admittedly autobiographical, should dramatize himself as a series of characters in Compton Mackenzie's autobiographical novels. Fitzgerald's offhand remark
suggests the manner in which he perhaps unconsciously "borrowed"
from Mackenzie.

In the early part of 1918, Fitzgerald wrote to Wilson: "In everything except my romantic Chestertonian orthodoxy I still agree with

[32] F. Scott Fitzgerald, "Letters to Friends," *The Crack-Up*, p. 247.
[33] *Ibid.*, p. 248.
[34] *Ibid.* Mrs. Katherine Fullerton Gerould's "British Novelists, Ltd." first appeared
in the *Yale Review* (VII [October, 1917]). Mrs. Gerould discussed two groups of
novelists: Wells, Bennett, and Galsworthy as the "elder brothers" of the "younger
fry," Hugh Walpole, J. D. Beresford, Compton Mackenzie, Gilbert Cannan, Oliver
Onions, and W. L. George. Mrs. Gerould was not particularly hard on Wells, and
thought *The Research Magnificent* a particularly outstanding work. Fitzgerald's opinion
that she underestimated Wells is testimony to the intensity of his early enthusiasm
for the author. Mrs. Gerould's objection to the "younger fry" as a whole was not
the lack of form in their novels, but rather the lack of morals in their heroes (pp.
179–80): "They are guilty of a lot of very ignoble impulses, and proceed often to
gratify them... What these young men and young women do is to call anything
virtuous that they happen to want to do." It is surprising that this attitude did not
draw comment from Fitzgerald. Mrs. Gerould's conclusion showed that she was
definitely of the saturation temperament (p. 185): "The time is ripe, once more,
I believe, for a few big picaresque novels."

the early Wells on human nature and the 'no hope for Tono Bungay' theory."[35] From all these numerous enthusiastic references to Wells, it is evident that, at the time Fitzgerald was writing *This Side of Paradise*, the authors he read, studied, and worshipped the most were *saturation* novelists: Wells and Mackenzie—Wells, who had become the spokesman and theorist for the "discursive" novel, and Mackenzie, who had been analyzed at some length by James as one of the outstanding practitioners of the novel of "documentation." Moreover, in the light of Fitzgerald's enthusiastic statement about *Boon*, it seems likely that Fitzgerald would have, had he had the opportunity, supported Wells in his controversy with James. At least Fitzgerald was familiar with a bit of the theory as well as a number of the examples of the *saturation* novel; and (if we may trust the reading lists of Amory Blaine in *This Side of Paradise*) he was familiar with a bit of the theory and perhaps a few of the examples of the novels of selection.[36] And his preference was definitely for *saturation*.

But probably the most revealing evidence concerning the influences on *This Side of Paradise* is in the book itself: "First, and partly by accident, they [Amory and his comrades] struck on certain books, a definite type of biographical novel that Amory christened quest books. In the quest book the hero set off in life armed with the best weapons and avowedly intending to use them as such weapons are usually used, to push their possessors ahead as selfishly and blindly as possible, but the heroes of the quest books discovered that there might be a more magnificent use for them. 'None Other Gods,' 'Sinister Street,' and 'The Research Magnificent' were examples of such books..." (131)[37] In this passage Fitzgerald described a particular species or pattern of the saturation novel – a pattern, moreover, that he followed in his own novel. Amory Blaine fills the requirements exactly as Fitzgerald sets them forth for the hero of the "quest" book. He starts out in life endowed with good looks and intelligence, determined to "push ahead as selfishly and blindly as possible." But he gradually looses his aristocratic attitude and, at the end of the book, is talking socialism – almost convincingly. He has found a "more magnificent use" for his "weapons."

[35] *Ibid.*, p. 252.

[36] It is a debatable point whether the reading lists – that is, the lists of books which are given at different stages of Amory's development to indicate his reading habits – in *This Side of Paradise* (New York: Charles Scribner's Sons, 1920) are actually reliable as indications of what Fitzgerald had read. But there appears the title of *A Portrait of the Artist as a Young Man* (p. 224), which James surely would have classified as a novel of selection, and there appears once the name of Conrad (p. 233).

[37] Location of quotations from *This Side of Paradise* will be identified in the text by page number in parentheses.

This "quest book" pattern is revealed in Fitzgerald's internal titles: the first book of *This Side of Paradise* is called "The Romantic Egotist," and the second "The Education of a Personage." The title of the last chapter of the book indicates the appropriate conversion: "The Egotist Becomes a Personage."

Since Fitzgerald, in defining the quest book, seems to be talking about the nature of his own work, it is revealing to take a closer look at the books which he gives as examples from which the pattern was cut. Robert Hugh Benson's *None Other Gods* (1911) fulfills, in the worst possible way, all of the requirements of the saturation novel.[38] It is a novel with a purpose – a vehicle for church propaganda. It is full of improperly motivated events: at one point, the father and brother of the hero are killed in an automobile accident in order to make the hero, Frank Guiseley, the heir to the title and estate. The author does not hesitate at any time to intrude for a "moral" chat with the reader. He explains fully the functions of his characters: "In short, the Rector plays no great part in this drama beyond that of a discreet, and mostly silent, Greek chorus of unimpeachable character." He states whether or not he agrees with the opinions of the characters: after a speech by one of them, Benson asserts: "(and in this explanation I think he was quite correct.)" And he admits, in one revealing passage, to stuffing (or *saturating*) his novel. After rather full treatment of an incident in which the hero, Frank, is cured of a serious illness by a Dr. Whitty, Benson says, "I scarcely know why I have included it in this book. But I was able to put it together from various witnesses, documentary and personal, and it seemed a pity to leave it out."[39] To be saturated, said James, was to be documented. Benson's statement is a full confession of the absence of a standard of relevance. But he does not even argue that the incident makes his story more life-like: the event simply happened, and could be reconstructed. For these reasons, he goes out of his way to admit, it was included.

The Research Magnificent, one of Wells's saturation novels, purports to be the reconstruction of the life of William Benham, who has bequeathed his papers to one White, a journalist. In this book Wells has prepared the reader for the qualities of the saturation novel by adopting

[38] Robert Hugh Benson, *None Other Gods* (St. Louis: B. Herder, 1911). Robert Hugh Benson is a now forgotten novelist and this novel is practically unobtainable. But Fitzgerald must have found Benson an interesting and somehow important novelist, for he mentions him at least two other times in Amory Blaine's reading lists in *This Side of Paradise* (pp. 57 and 285). *None Other Gods* is, by any standards, a very poor novel and deserves to be forgotten.

[39] Robert Hugh Benson, *None Other Gods*, pp. 61–271.

White as his narrator and, in turn, portraying White as sorting and evaluating a vast quantity of shapeless material: "This collection of papers was not a story, not an essay, not a confession, not a diary. It was – nothing definable. It went into no conceivable covers.... It wanted even a title."[40] As a result, *The Research Magnificent* is in part more essay than fiction, more rhetoric than art. It is as though it were not a novel acting as a vehicle for certain ideas, but rather a set of ideas on which a novel has been insecurely grafted. William Benham conquers in turn the "limits" of Fear, Indulgence, Jealousy, and Prejudice. The allegorical nature of the volume would not have been more apparent had Wells even used these abstractions as names for his characters. *The Research Magnificent* fulfills in every way the definition of the saturation novel. It provides Wells with an opportunity to discuss social problems, it is discursive, full of irrelevance, and it has the "personal outbreaks" of the author.

Although both *None Other Gods* and *The Research Magnificent* were important to Fitzgerald, the third volume which he listed as a "quest" book, *Sinister Street*, was by far the most influential on and acted most as the model for *This Side of Paradise*. And *Sinister Street*, as James said, of all the saturation novels "can... scarce have helped being the most sufficient in itself."[41] James noted that there was in Compton Mackenzie "an unexpected amount of talent and life" but that there was "a considerable or large element of waste and irresponsibility – *selection* isn't in him."[42] Probably James's remarks about Mackenzie's "lively talent of the memoriser"[43] stung Mackenzie to reply in his "Epilogical Letter to John Nicolas Mavrogordato" at the end of *Sinister Street*. In this letter Mackenzie significantly revealed his intentions in the novel. He began: "There has lately been noticeable in the press a continuous suggestion that the modern novel is thinly disguised autobiography; and since the lives of most men are peculiarly formless this suggestion has been amplified into an attack upon the form of the novel." He noted that "many critics have persisted in regarding 'Youth's Encounter' [the title of the first book in *Sinister Street*] merely as an achievement of memory." This was precisely James's charge. Mackenzie answered, "If I were to set down all I could remember of my childhood, the book would not by this time have reached much beyond my fifth year." Mackenzie seems to be arguing that, since he could have put more in

[40] H. G. Wells, *The Research Magnificent* (New York: The Macmillan Company, 1915), p. 9.
[41] James, "The New Novel," *op. cit.*, p. 361.
[42] James, *Letters*, II, 365.
[43] James, "The New Novel," *op. cit.*, p. 361.

and didn't, he must have used "selection" – the selection for which
James pleaded. But Mackenzie thought of selection, as did Wells, as
omission or addition rather than as method, or the "art of figuring
synthetically." Probably with James's remarks about the necessity for
a "pointed intention" well in mind, Mackenzie proceeded to define
the "theme" of *Sinister Street*: "The theme of these two stories is the
youth of a man who presumably will be a priest." But how, one might
well ask, is the theme differentiated from the story; what is the basis
of relevance established by this broad statement of the theme? Evidently *relevance* was to Mackenzie a very real problem, for he said, "I
am tempted to hope that with the publication of the second volume
many irrelevancies have established their relevancy." Since he did not
say *all* irrelevancies, it seems fair to conclude that Mackenzie himself
was aware of a number which would remain, and for these he offered
no defense. Indeed, when he said "I have given you as fully as I could
the various influences that went to mold him [Michael Fane],"[44] he
seemed proud of the bulk, the quantity – all 1156 pages of it. Mackenzie was a prime example of the documentary novelist. And *Sinister Street*,
the most saturated of the *saturation* novels, was the closest model for *This
Side of Paradise*.

Edmund Wilson, a close friend of F. Scott Fitzgerald from their
Princeton days and in a position to be familiar with Fitzgerald's literary
enthusiasms, said in 1922 that Fitzgerald, when he wrote *This Side of
Paradise*, "was drunk with Compton Mackenzie, and the book sounds
like an American attempt to rewrite 'Sinister Street.'" Mackenzie, said
Wilson, "lacks both the intellectual force and the emotional imagination to give body and outline to the material which he secretes in such
enormous abundance."[45] Some of the reviewers of *This Side of Paradise*
noted its resemblance to *Sinister Street*. The reviewer for *The New Republic*
said that Fitzgerald wrote his novel with "an acquisitive eye on Sinister
Street and The Research Magnificent."[46] Frances Newman, in the
Atlanta Constitution, drew so many parallels between *This Side of Paradise*
and *Sinister Street* that Fitzgerald felt forced to reply in the first letter
he had "ever written to a critic." As this letter gives Fitzgerald's own
views as to the relation between *This Side of Paradise* and *Sinister Street*,
it deserves close scrutiny. Fitzgerald asserted, "While it astonished me

[44] Compton Mackenzie, *Sinister Street* (New York: D. Appleton and Company,
1919), pp. 655–57.
[45] Edmund Wilson, "The Literary Spotlight: F. Scott Fitzgerald," *The Bookman*,
LV (March, 1922), 21.
[46] R. V. A. S., "This Side of Paradise," *The New Republic*, XXII (May 12, 1920),
362.

that so few critics mentioned the influence of Sinister Street on This Side of Paradise, I feel sure that it was much more in intention than in literal fact." It had occurred to him "to write an American version of the history of that sort of young man," but he "was hindered by lack of perspective as well as by congenital short-comings." He pointed out the remarkable resemblance between his life and that of Michael Fane (the hero of *Youth's Encounter* and *Sinister Street*), which even his friends had noticed: "I have five copies of Youth's Encounter at present in my library, sent me by people who stumbled on the book and thought that it was an amazing parallel to my own life." Fitzgerald admitted that when he began *This Side of Paradise* at the age of twenty-one, his "literary taste was so unformed" that *Youth's Encounter* was still his "perfect book." And he added, "My book quite naturally shows the influence to a marked degree." It was surely not in terms of subject matter exclusively that Fitzgerald thought of *Youth's Encounter* as the perfect book. Its structure must have appealed to him too – and the form (or marked lack thereof) was that of the *saturation* novel. Indeed, when Fitzgerald said that his book showed the influence of Mackenzie's, he must have been thinking primarily of technique rather than subject matter, for the remainder of his letter to the reviewer was devoted to showing how the parallels between characters and events which Frances Newman had drawn were invalid in that parallels existed also between the characters and events of *This Side of Paradise* and the people and happenings of real life, within Fitzgerald's own experience.

It was these detailed parallels in Miss Newman's review which Fitzgerald resented. Monsignor Darcy was "my best friend, the Monsignor Sigorney Fay, to whom the book was dedicated," rather than Father Viner in *Sinister Street*. As proof, Fitzgerald said that "the letters in the book are almost transcriptions of his own letters to me." Beatrice, Amory Blaine's mother, was "an actual character, the mother of a friend of mine, whose name I cannot mention," and not the mother of Michael Fane. John Peale Bishop was the model for Thomas P. D'Invilliers, and not the "dilettante aesthete Wilmot from Mackenzie." And, of course, Fitzgerald might have noted that Amory Blaine was F. Scott Fitzgerald and not Mackenzie's Michael Fane. Fitzgerald added, "You seem to be unconscious that even Mackenzie had his sources such as Dorian Grey and None Other Gods and that occasionally we may have drunk at the same springs."[47] Undoubtedly several common sources were possible; to *Dorian Grey* and *None Other Gods*

[47] Frances Newman, *Letters*, ed. by Hansell Baugh (New York: Horace Liveright, 1929), pp. 40–42.

might be added any one of a number of Wells novels. Certainly the tradition of the *saturation* novel was firmly enough established to have exerted influence independently on Mackenzie and Fitzgerald.

It is not worth the effort, and probably not even possible, to determine in specific detail the borrowings Fitzgerald made from *Sinister Street*. It is enough to know that *This Side of Paradise* was deeply influenced by it both in form and matter. The form of *Sinister Street*, as James pointed out, was that of the so-called "slice-of-life" novel, or, more particularly, of that species of it which Fitzgerald called the "quest" book. *This Side of Paradise* fulfills the requirements of that form as set forth by Wells. The characterization of Amory Blaine, and not a continuous action, is the center of interest, and this emphasis on character allows for the "felt" of irrelevancies which Wells considered necessary to make the novel life-like. *This Side of Paradise* even has the intrusive author which Wells defended; and the latter part of the book, devoted to debates on capitalism and socialism, is certainly utilized as a vehicle for the discussion of social problems.

III. A GESTURE OF INDEFINITE REVOLT

Fitzgerald once referred to an early version of *This Side of Paradise* as a "picaresque ramble" or a "prose, modernistic Childe Harolde,"[48] terms which well describe the episodic nature of his novel. There is no continuous line of action but rather a series of episodes related one to the other by Amory Blaine, the central character. The story is the biography of Amory Blaine during the formative years of his life. The episodes are related in that they constitute collectively the education of the hero, but there is no single plot-line to unify the novel. Such a loose structure lends itself well to documentation: an abundance of detailed incidents may be included so long as they revolve around the hero. As the reviewer for the *Publisher's Weekly* said – "It isn't a story in the regular sense: there's no beginning, except the beginning of Amory Blaine, born healthy, wealthy and extraordinarily good-looking, and by way of being spoiled by a restless mother whom he quaintly calls by her first name, Beatrice. There's no middle to the story, except the eager fumbling at life of this same handsome boy, proud, clean-minded, born to conquer yet fumbling, at college and in love with Isabelle, then Clara, then Rosalind, then Eleanor. No end to the story except the closing picture of this same boy in his early twenties, a bit less confident about life, with no God in his heart... his ideas still in

---

[48] Fitzgerald, "Letters to Friends," *The Crack-Up*, p. 252.

riot."[49] With no central action, the book can have no beginning, middle, or end in the conventional sense.

Henry James's great demand for the novel was a center of interest or a motivating idea. Taking his cue from James, Percy Lubbock asserted that a novel "cannot begin to take shape" until it has "a subject, one and whole and irreducible... for its support." The question the critic must pose is "what the novel in his hand is about. What was the novelist's intention, in a phrase?" If the novel's "subject" cannot be stated in a phrase, if it is not "expressible in ten words that reveal its unity," then the critic can proceed no further. "The form of the book depends on it, and until it is known there is nothing to be said of the form."[50] It was with a note of contempt that Wells had said of James, "The thing his novel is *about* is always there."[51] This *relevance*, thought Wells, deprived the novel of "life."

What, we may well ask, is *This Side of Paradise* about? Edmund Wilson asserted that, as a consequence of its deriving so much from *Sinister Street*, "Amory Blaine... had a very poor chance for coherence... he was... an uncertain quantity in a phantasmagoria of incident which had no dominating intention to endow it with unity and force." Wilson concluded, "In short, 'This Side of Paradise' is really not *about* anything; intellectually it amounts to little more than a gesture – a gesture of indefinite revolt."[52] By definition the saturation novel is not about any one thing: it is about "life" and must, therefore, include those irrelevancies which prevent life itself from coming to a focus and being *about* something.

But, as James said, even the *slice* of life must have been *cut*; it cannot exist in an amorphous state. Even the *saturation* novel has technique of some kind, though the author may not have been conscious of its use. Contrary to Lubbock, therefore, one *can* talk about the form or technique of a novel whose subject is not reducible to a brief statement. The question is whether or not one can reduce the subject or theme of *This Side of Paradise* to some general terms on which to base a discussion of technique. Referring to a previous version of his novel (when it was entitled *The Romantic Egotist*), Fitzgerald once remarked, "I really believe that no one else could have written so searchingly the story of the youth of our generation."[53] It would seem safe to assume that much

---

[49] R. S. S., "Ernest Poole and Tarkington at their best," *The Publisher's Weekly* XCVII (April 17, 1920), 1289.
[50] Lubbock, *op. cit.*, p. 41.
[51] Wells, *Boon*, p. 109.
[52] Wilson, "The Literary Spotlight: F. Scott Fitzgerald," *op. cit.*, pp. 21–22.
[53] Fitzgerald, "Letters to Friends," *The Crack-Up*, p. 252.

of the same intention of method and theme implicit in this remark carried over into the published work. To this "story of the youth of our generation" might be added Wilson's phrase, "a gesture of indefinite revolt." If we acknowledge that *This Side of Paradise* is *about* the obscurely motivated and vaguely directed rebellion of the youth of Fitzgerald's generation, we may not have discovered a precise and lucid "pointed intention," but we do have a basis for analysis and evaluation.

Granting *This Side of Paradise* its method of *saturation* we can still critically examine its technique. Indeed, most critics have agreed that the crucial failure in the book was the failure of Fitzgerald to see his material objectively – that is, a failure in point of view. Fitzgerald has adopted no machinery as an integral part of his story whose function it is to evaluate the characters and the incidents. The story is told from the point of view of the hero, Amory Blaine, and the reader is left with Blaine's judgment unless Fitzgerald, by implication or by direct intervention, indicates otherwise. The general impression left with the reader, after he has finished the book, is as Paul Rosenfeld put it, that Fitzgerald "does not sustainedly perceive his girls and men for what they are, and tends to invest them with precisely the glamour with which they in pathetic assurance rather childishly invest themselves."[54]

Fitzgerald was, of course, young and immature when he wrote his novel, and, in writing about himself, was frequently unable to see his material objectively. The critical problem, however, is to discover what, in the book, betrays Fitzgerald's moral position. Some of the most revealing passages as to the author's attitude appear in the stage directions of the scenes done in play form, in which the author, because of his choice of method, is forced to speak in his own person. Fitzgerald does not confine himself to mere description; he seizes the opportunity for little chats with and asides to the reader. He betrays something of his whole position and attitude in the opening stage directions for the Amory-Rosalind meeting scene. In setting the scene, he first describes Rosalind's excessively pink and luxurious bedroom and enumerates the items laid out for Rosalind's debut. He then says confidentially to the reader: "One would enjoy seeing the bill called forth by the finery displayed and one is possessed by a desire to see the princess for whose benefit – Look! There's some one! Disappointment!" (179) It turns out to be only the maid. Fitzgerald obviously expects the reader to be as awed as he by the expensive scene which he has painted. He seems to expect the material wealth displayed to suffice for the reader to invest the characters, not even introduced yet, with intense interest and

[54] Paul Rosenfeld, "F. Scott Fitzgerald," *The Crack-Up*, p. 319.

glamour. He does indeed seem blinded by the glitter of his own costly creation.

When Rosalind does enter, Fitzgerald asserts on her behalf: "In the true sense she is not spoiled. Her fresh enthusiasm, her will to grow and learn, her endless faith in the inexhaustibility of romance, her courage and fundamental honesty – these things are not spoiled." (183) One might question Fitzgerald's emphasis of her romantic rather than realistic nature when, in fact, she turns down Amory, whom she presumably loves, because he has no money, and exclaims "'I can't be shut away from the trees and flowers, cooped up in a little flat, waiting for you.'" Her "endless faith" in romance turns out to be a horror of household duties and an egocentric craving for luxury: "'I don't want to think about pots and kitchens and brooms. I want to worry whether my legs will get slick and brown when I swim in the summer.'" (209–10) Fitzgerald is so entranced by the beauty and riches he has portrayed that he seems unable to comprehend Rosalind's fundamental selfishness and superficiality. The portrayal of Rosalind is, technically, a failure in characterization. For Fitzgerald attributes qualities to her which are mutually exclusive. His assertion that Rosalind is not spoiled is in conflict with the way he portrays her as acting. Fitzgerald closes the meeting scene: "And deep under the aching sadness that will pass in time, Rosalind feels that she has lost something, she knows not what, she knows not why." (211) The tone is all wrong, for it assumes a depth for Rosalind which, by this time, the reader knows she is incapable of achieving; these closing pretentious if somewhat lyrical phrases seem to be an attempt to surround her with a poetry which she does not deserve.

Because Rosalind rejects him, Amory goes on a drunken spree, and during one of his brief moments of sobriety, bewails his great loss:

"My own girl – my own – Oh –"
He clinched his teeth so that the tears streamed in a flood from his eyes.
"Oh... my baby girl, all I had, all I wanted!... Oh, my girl, come back, come back! I need you... need you... We're so pitiful ...just misery we brought each other... She'll be shut away from me... I can't see her; I can't be her friend. It's got to be that way – it's got to be –"
And then again:
"We've been so happy, so very happy..." (216)

Perhaps Amory is so affected by his broken love affair that he could talk in this sophomoric fashion. The effect of this speech on the reader, contrary to what Fitzgerald seems to expect, is one of embarrassment – embarrassment for the novelist. And when he says that there had been "so much dramatic tragedy" for Amory, one is convinced that Fitzgerald has attempted and expected an effect which he does not get. What the reader has seen is certainly not tragedy and not very good drama.

Again, in preparing the scene for the meeting of Eleanor and Amory, Fitzgerald's diction and imagery suggest an attempt at dramatic profundity which does not succeed:

> But Eleanor – did Amory dream her? Afterward their ghosts played, yet both of them hoped from their souls never to meet. Was it the infinite sadness of her eyes that drew him or the mirror of himself that he found in the gorgeous clarity of her mind? She will have no other adventure like Amory, and if she reads this she will say:
> "And Amory will have no other adventure like me." (238)

The tone created by Fitzgerald's language is struggling for a far more serious effect than is actually achieved in the scene. And when Eleanor and Amory take their final parting, Fitzgerald writes:

> Their poses were strewn about the pale dawn like broken glass. The stars were long gone and there were left only the little sighing gusts of wind and the silences between... but naked souls are poor things ever, and soon he turned homeward and let new lights come in with the sun. (258)

The dramatic details and images, like those of the beginning of this scene, betray the romantic haze through which Fitzgerald conceived his characters and their struggles.

Fitzgerald's inability to remain detached and uninvolved interferred, naturally, with the development of the theme of *This Side of Paradise*. In order that the revolt of his generation be made comprehensible and convincing, it was imperative that Fitzgerald present his youth objectively. The precise nature of the revolt undertaken by the youth never clearly emerges. There is, presumably, a "questioning aloud the institutions" (131) of all phases of American life, including educational, religious, political, and moral. But the questioning remains submerged, only half articulated, lost in a multitude of cross purposes.

Much of the "revolt" seems on the periphery rather than at the center of the novel. There is Burne Holiday's objection to the social system represented by the clubs at Princeton. But this "did not seem such a vital subject as it had in the two years before" (134) to Amory. There is Amory's periodic religious questioning. In a letter to Tom D'Invilliers after the war he says, "I confess that the war instead of making me orthodox, which is the correct reaction, has made me a passionate agnostic....This crisis-inspired religion is rather valueless and fleeting at best." (176) And at the end of the book, the reader is told that "there was no God in his [Amory's] heart." (304) Even in the long monologue in which Amory presents the case for socialism to the Capitalist and his Sycophant (Mr. Ferrenby and Garvin are more symbols than characters), it is all on the spur of the moment and the theories which Amory expresses are mixed up in his mind with "the richest man [getting]... the most beautiful girl if he wants her." (299)

But the aspect of the revolt best remembered is the "questioning of moral codes." (66) Fitzgerald wrote of his generation: "None of the Victorian mothers – and most of the mothers were Victorians – had any idea how casually their daughters were accustomed to be kissed." (64) The "revolt" seldom goes much beyond the kiss. When Amory goes on his trip with the Princeton musical comedy, he sees "girls doing things that even in his memory would have been impossible." (65) And what are these acts that seem so shocking? "Eating three o'clock, after-dance suppers in impossible cafes, talking of every side of life with an air half of earnestness, half of mockery, yet with a furtive excitement that Amory considered stood for a real moral let-down." (65)

Yet, in Amory's own case, there seems to be an ambivalent attitude developed toward sex. There is in him an extreme daring (for the year 1920); but also a recurring aversion. As his first love affair just reaches a climax in a kiss, "sudden revulsion seized Amory, disgust, loathing for the whole incident. He desired frantically to be away, never to see Myra again, never to kiss any one." (15) Amory is given "a puzzled, furtive interest in everything concerning sex" (20) but his repugnance of sex seems to be a fixed and uncontrollable part of his reaction. When he and Fred Sloane are spending what was meant to be a wild evening out with a couple of girls, Amory thinks he sees a pale man watching him. Up in the girls' apartment, just as "temptation [is creeping]... over him like a warm wind," (122) he sees the vision again, whereupon he abruptly leaves and runs into an alley, where "before his eyes a face flashed... a face pale and distorted with a sort of infinite evil that twisted it like flame in the wind; *but he knew, for the half instant that the gong tanged and hummed, that it was the face of Dick Humbird.*" (126) Dick Humbird was Amory's friend at Princeton who had been killed in an automobile accident; Amory had been riding in another car and had seen the wreck and Dick's body shortly after the accident. In this ambiguous

fashion Amory connects sex not only with evil but also with death. The
terrifying evil which surrounds sex for Amory is extended to encompass
beauty also: "Eleanor was, say, the last time that evil crept close to
Amory under the mask of beauty." (238) Yet Eleanor is treated as a
pure, poetic influence on Amory. And when Amory, near the end of
the book, attempts to assess the meaning of his experience, he discovers
that sex and beauty have become inextricably mixed with evil: "The
problem of evil had solidified for Amory into the problem of sex....
Inseparably linked with evil was beauty.... Amory knew that every time
he had reached toward it longingly it had leered out at him with the
grotesque face of evil." (302) Although this development in Amory of
a puritan-like sensibility does not let him serve well as a symbol of
revolt, the novel perhaps gains in value from the increased complexity
and subtlety in the presentation of his character.

At one point in his story, Amory cries out, "My whole generation is
restless." (99) The novel is more a representation of that restlessness
than it is a coherent assertion of revolt. Perhaps that is why Edmund
Wilson characterized the novel as a "gesture of indefinite revolt." Just
what constitutes the revolt is not readily apparent; what is being revolted *against* does not clearly emerge. But it is because of the vague re-
belliousness or "restlessness" in it that *This Side of Paradise* retains importance in literary history. It stands at the beginning of a decade
famed for its literature of revolt. It is the first of the post-war novels by
the then new generation of authors, the generation which had "grown
up to find all Gods dead, all wars fought, all faiths in man shaken."
(304) As Alfred Kazin has said, *This Side of Paradise* "announced the
lost generation."[55] In spite of the apparently blurred and mixed purposes in the novel, the sexual, social, and literary restlessness of the
younger generation came through clear enough to capture the imagination of a decade.

The point of view in *This Side of Paradise*, is, in one sense, conventional. The author assumes omniscience but visualizes most of the story
through the eyes of the protagonist, Amory Blaine. After the opening
of the book, presenting a summary of Amory's background and a brief
outline of the life of Beatrice O'Hara, Amory's mother, Fitzgerald
maintains the focus rather steadily on Amory. Although no scenes are
represented at which Amory is not present, when it suits his purpose
Fitzgerald does not hesitate to relate what is going on in the minds of
characters other than Amory. For example, in the first of the many love

[55] Alfred Kazin, *On Native Grounds* (New York: Reynal & Hitchcock, 1942), p. 316.

scenes in the book, when Myra St. Claire is seated with Amory before the fire in the Country Club, Fitzgerald confides: "Myra's eyes became dreamy. What a story this would make to tell Marylyn! Here on the couch with this *wonderful*-looking boy – the little fire – the sense that they were alone in the great building." (15) This scene of adolescent love is no doubt enriched by this dialogue of Myra's secret response – her acute consciousness of the drama in which she is playing a part. Although there are a few instances of this kind in the novel, it is Amory's mind which is portrayed predominantly. Inasmuch as the story is a history of his "education," it is appropriate that the reader observe Amory's development both externally and internally.

Fitzgerald may well be charged with crudity for a number of instances in his manipulation of point of view. He indulged in the more or less conventional form of author-intervention in which the author presents directly to the reader facts which only he and the reader share. The characterization of Amory at the end of his student days at St. Regis may serve as an example:

> He was changed as completely as Amory Blaine could ever be changed. Amory plus Beatrice plus two years in Minneapolis – these had been his ingredients when he entered St. Regis'. But the Minneapolis years were not a thick enough overlay to conceal the "Amory plus Beatrice" from the ferreting eyes of a boarding-school, so St. Regis' had very painfully drilled Beatrice out of him, and begun to lay down new and more conventional planking on the fundamental Amory. But both St. Regis' and Amory were unconscious of the fact that this fundamental Amory had not in himself changed. Those qualities for which he had suffered, his moodiness, his tendency to pose, his laziness, and his love of playing the fool, were not taken as a matter of course...(35)

There is an alternative to Fitzgerald's method in this passage, one which Fitzgerald himself was to be acutely conscious of later when he wrote in large letters in his notes for *The Last Tycoon*, "ACTION IS CHARACTER."[56] Instead of summarizing Amory's character in general and abstract terms, Fitzgerald might have portrayed Amory by dramatic representation of his thoughts and actions. The above passage one might expect to find in a novelist's notebook, as the embryo of a number of ideas to be worked out in detail. Indeed, later in *This Side of Paradise*, in regular notebook fashion, Fitzgerald analyzes Amory's character by simple enumeration:

[56] F. Scott Fitzgerald, *The Last Tycoon* (New York: Charles Scribner's Sons, 1941), p. 163.

If his [Amory's] reaction to his environment could be tabulated, the chart would have appeared like this, beginning with his earliest years:
1. The fundamental Amory.
2. Amory plus Beatrice.
3. Amory plus Beatrice plus Minneapolis.
Then St. Regis' had pulled him to pieces and started him over again:
4. Amory plus St. Regis'.
5. Amory plus St. Regis' plus Princeton.
That had been his nearest approach to success through conformity. The fundamental Amory, idle, imaginative, rebellious, had been nearly snowed under. He had conformed, he had succeeded, but as his imagination was neither satisfied nor grasped by his own success, he had listlessly, half-accidentally chucked the whole thing and become again:
6. The fundamental Amory. (108–09)

This method of presenting character, in enumerated, general terms, in a direct address from author to reader, is surely less effective and convincing than the alternative of dramatic representation. The reader is deprived of his privileged experience of *inferring* and *drawing conclusions* from interpretation and analysis of action.

But Fitzgerald intrudes in his story also in a much more real sense. There are in *This Side of Paradise* a number of personal outbreaks of the kind that Wells thought gave depth and "subjective reality" to a novel. When Amory imagines wives, whom he had known as debutantes, looking at him and wishing that they had married him instead of their husbands, Fitzgerald cries out at him: "Oh, the enormous conceit of the man!" (160) Occasionally Fitzgerald's enthusiasm or boundless energy carries him directly into his novel, in the first person singular. In his treatment of the affair between Amory and Eleanor, Fitzgerald begins: "Eleanor hated Maryland passionately. She belonged to the oldest of the old families of Ramilly County and lived in a big, gloomy house with her grandfather. She had been born and brought up in France... I see I am starting wrong. Let me begin again." (239) And Fitzgerald does begin again – with Amory. It would appear that Fitzgerald becomes aware in mid-paragraph that he has shifted his point of view. In recasting the scene, he first portrays Amory's meeting with Eleanor and later allows Amory (and the reader) to learn Eleanor's history and background from his aunt and from Eleanor herself. By this method he maintains consistently Amory's point of view. It is difficult to justify the old and actually discarded "beginning" in the novel, followed by Fitzgerald's personal reference to his technique.

Much that he gained by improving his method he lost by retaining the false start.

Another instance of direct intrusion by the author occurs when Fitzgerald suggests that neither Eleanor nor Amory was capable of enduring love at the time of their meeting; he speculates "I suppose that was why they turned to Brooke, and Swinburne, and Shelley." (248) Capable of omniscience, Fitzgerald suddenly discovers that his knowledge is limited, and he *supposes* when he might instead *assert*. It would be difficult, if not impossible, to justify Fitzgerald's somewhat intrusive lines; it is certainly not the bold intrusion which Wells advocated.

One aspect of the point of view in *This Side of Paradise* has attracted the attention of a number of the book's critics. The reviewer for *The Nation* referred to "impressionistic episodes"[57] in the book, while the reviewer for *The New Republic* said that the novel follows "in general technique what we might call the Impressionistic Novel shadowed forth in James Joyce's Portrait of the Artist as a Young Man."[58] More recently (in 1935) Harlan Hatcher asserted that *This Side of Paradise* was ultra-modern in technique, utilizing the impressionistic style then in its first flower through the success of James Joyce's *Portrait of the Artist as a Young Man.*"[59] As late as 1941, Oscar Cargill spoke of Fitzgerald's "effort to do school life as realistically as Joyce had done it in *A Portrait of the Artist as a Young Man.*"[60] There were elements of tech-

---

[57] "Reforms and Beginnings," *The Nation*, LX (April 24, 1920), 558.

[58] R. V. A. S., "This Side of Paradise," *op. cit.*, p. 362.

[59] Harlan Hatcher, *Creating the Modern American Novel* (New York: Farrar & Rinehart, 1935), p. 80.

[60] Cargill, *op. cit.*, p. 349. Mr. Cargill implies that Joyce's early novel was the model for *This Side of Paradise*. He states flatly (p. 349): "One might not suspect this from reading *This Side of Paradise*, which seems more of a travesty than a serious effort, yet such is the case." There is indication in *This Side of Paradise* that Fitzgerald had read Joyce's novel. He says at one point of Amory (*This Side of Paradise*, p. 224): "He was puzzled and depressed by 'A Portrait of the Artist as a Young Man'..." And there are certain lines of action in the two books which are similar: the detailed account of unhappy school life, the growing interest in literature, and the rejection of religion – in both cases, Catholicism. There is even an echo of Joyce's famous phrase (*A Portrait of the Artist as a Young Man* ["The Modern Library"; New York: Random House, 1928], p. 299), "... to forge in the smithy of my soul the uncreated conscience of my race," in Fitzgerald's novel. Amory tells Tom D'Invilliers (*This Side of Paradise*, p. 230) that he "represent[s] the critical consciousness of the race," and he refers to himself, near the end of the book (p. 285), as "preserved to help in building up the living consciousness of the race." The phrases are different, of course, but there is enough similarity to suggest unconscious borrowing. However, there is no indication that Fitzgerald was consciously imitating Joyce's book; *A Portrait* was too much a novel of selection for Fitzgerald's taste at the time. He was, like Amory, probably "puzzled" by it.

nique beyond the conventional in *This Side of Paradise* that convinced
reviewers and critics that it was "ultra-modern" in method.

Probably one of the factors that caused this impression was the abundance of poetry in the book. Most of the poetry is presented in the
conventional way, as written by various of the characters, but some of
it is presented in the novel manner of prose exposition, often set off
from the surrounding text and calling attention to itself by appearing
in italics. At the end of Book One, as Amory is leaving Princeton, Fitzgerald writes:

> The last light fades and drifts across the land – the low, long
> land; the sunny land of spires; the ghosts of evening tune again
> their lyres and wander singing in a plaintive band down the long
> corridors of trees; pale fires echo the night from tower top to tower:
> oh, sleep that dreams, and dream that never tires, press from the
> petals of the lotus flower something of this to keep, the essence of
> an hour.
> No more to wait the twilight of the moon in this sequestered vale
> of star and spire, for one eternal morning of desire passes to time
> and earthy afternoon. Here, Heroclitus, did you find in fire and
> shifting things the prophecy you hurled down the dead years; this
> midnight my desire will see, shadowed among the embers, furled
> in flame, the splendor and the sadness of the world. (168)

Presumably these images are drifting through Amory's mind as he
contemplates the close of one stage of his life and vaguely anticipates
the beginning of another. The technique is a kind of poetical and highly
compact, rather than discursive, stream-of-consciousness.

Fitzgerald utilizes a variation of this technique in a scene describing
Amory's return, late at night from an evening in New York to Princeton:

> So the gray car crept nightward in the dark and there was no
> life stirred as it went by.... As the still ocean paths before the shark
> in starred and glittering waterways, beauty-high, the moon-
> swathed trees divided, pair on pair on pair, while flapping night
> birds cried across the air....
> A moment by an inn of lamps and shades, a yellow inn under
> a yellow moon – then silence, where crescendo laughter fades...
> the car swung out again to the winds of June, mellowed the
> shadows where the distance grew, then crushed the yellow shadows
> into blue.... (94)

This passage, also set off in italics, is introduced as "the ghost of two
stanzas of a poem forming" in Amory's mind as he rides through the

night with his half-drunken companions. These images vaguely drifting
through Amory's consciousness are to be rapidly dissolved as his party
has the sobering experience of coming upon the wrecked automobile
of their companions, one of whom – Dick Humbird – is dead. Again,
the effect of this technique is that of a highly compact and selective
stream-of-consciousness. The vague beauty of the poetry serves as a
stark contrast to the sudden glare of "tragedy's emerald eyes."

A number of interesting technical devices are used near the end of
This Side of Paradise, in the last chapter, "The Egotist Becomes a Personage." As the title suggests, Fitzgerald is concerned with representing
a major development in the character of his protagonist. In the last
section (called "The Collapse of Several Pillars") of the immediately
preceding chapter, Amory has learned in quick succession that the girl
he loves, Rosalind, has become engaged, that he can expect no more
money from the investments he has inherited, and that his great good
friend, Monsignor Darcy, is dead. This series of misfortunes precipitates
an internal conflict and "debate" in Amory. Fitzgerald, confronted
with the necessity of dramatizing Amory's mind at considerable length,
solves the problem by adopting a variety of techniques. Amory is portrayed first in New York on a rainy afternoon in front of a theater just
after the matinee has ended thinking about the lives of the people
passing him on the street. His thoughts are represented in a more or
less conventional "recording" of his wandering imagination:

> He pictured the rooms where these people lived – where the
> patterns of the blistered wall-papers were heavy reiterated sun-
> flowers on green and yellow backgrounds, where there were tin
> bathtubs and gloomy hallways and verdureless, unnamable spaces
> in back of the buildings; where even love dressed as seduction – a
> sordid murder around the corner, illicit motherhood in the flat
> above. And always there was the economical stuffiness of indoor
> winter, and the long summers, nightmares of perspiration be-
> tween sticky enveloping walls... dirty restaurants where careless,
> tired people helped themselves to sugar with their own used coffee-
> spoons, leaving hard brown deposits in the bowl. (275)

Amory's spontaneous vision of the poor of New York vanishes as he
moves away from the theater and takes a Fifth Avenue bus, on which
he begins to think about himself, and to confront himself with a series
of incontrovertible facts to understand and a number of decisions to
make. In representing Amory struggling with his own problem, Fitzgerald uses the device of internal voices: "Somewhere in his [Amory's]
mind a conversation began, rather resumed its place in his attention,"

a conversation "composed not of two voices, but of one, which acted alike as questioner and answerer" (276):

> Question. – Well – what's the situation?
> Answer. – That I have about twenty-four dollars to my name.
> Q. – You have the Lake Geneva estate.
> A. – But I intend to keep it.
> Q. – Can you live?
> A. – I can 't imagine not being able to. People make money in books and I've found that I can always do the things that people do in books. Really they are the only things I can do. (276)

This question-answer exploration of Amory's situation and condition concludes after about two pages, with the final unanswered question, "Q. – Where are you drifting?" (278)

In answer to this question of double significance Fitzgerald introduces a new technique: "This dialogue merged grotesquely into [Amory's] mind's most familiar state – a grotesque blending of desires, worries, exterior impressions and physical reactions." (278) Details of Amory's present experience on the bus begin to mix inextricably with vague recollections of his boyhood as present and past mingle and merge.

> One Hundred and Twenty-seventh Street–or One Hundred and Thirty-seventh Street... Two and three look alike–no, not much. Seat damp... are clothes absorbing wetness from seat, or seat absorbing dryness from clothes?... Sitting on wet substance gave appendicitis, so Froggy Parker's mother said. Well he'd had it–I'll sue the steamboat company, Beatrice said, and my uncle has a quarter interest–did Beatrice go to heaven?... probably not –He represented Beatrice's immortality, also love-affairs of numerous dead men who surely had never thought of him... if it wasn't appendicitis, influenza maybe. What? One Hundred and Twentieth Street? That must have been One Hundred and Twelfth back there. One O Two instead of One Two Seven. Rosalind not like Beatrice, Eleanor like Beatrice, only wilder and brainier. Apartments along here expensive–probably hundred and fifty a month– maybe two hundred. Uncle had only paid hundred a month for whole great big house in Minneapolis. Question–were the stairs on the left or right as you came in? Anyway, in 12 Univee they were straight back and to the left. What a dirty river–want to go down there and see if it's dirty–French rivers all brown or black, so were Southern rivers. Twenty-four dollars meant four hundred and eighty doughnuts. He could live on it three months and sleep in the park. Wonder where Jill was – Jill Bayne, Fayne, Sayne – what the devil – neck hurts, darned uncomfortable seat. No desire to sleep with Jill, what could Alec see in her? Alec had a coarse

taste in women. Own taste the best; Isabelle, Clara, Rosalind, Eleanor, were all-American. Eleanor would pitch, probably southpaw. Rosalind was outfield, wonderful hitter, Clara first base, maybe. Wonder what Humbird's body looked like now. If he himself hadn't been bayonet instructor he'd have gone up to line three months sooner, probably been killed. Where's the darned bell – (278–79)

As the stream-of-consciousness trails off at this point, Fitzgerald reverts to the conventional manner of representing Amory's thoughts. Although this passage appears aimless and meandering, it serves the function of dramatizing Amory at a crucial stage in his "education" when, in the face of an uncertain future, he is overwhelmed by the crowded memories of an ever-shifting past. The technique seems admirably suited to the demands of the narrative.

Fitzgerald's rapid transition, as in the passage above, from one technique to another, as it suits his narrative purpose, shows that he was familiar with and fairly adept in the use of a variety of methods. Some justification can be offered for his use of a specific technique for a specific situation: when Amory is contemplating the poor of the city, some control is needed to give his imaginative conception of their lives coherence and to lead logically into the examination of his own life; when he is sorting through his own problems, the question-answer method serves well to dramatize the uncertainties of his own mind; when he has posed for himself the unanswerable question, "Where are you drifting?" (with both physical and spiritual implications) the stream-of-consciousness method, with all of its discursiveness, serves well to dramatize the blending of those "desires, worries, exterior impressions and physical reactions" (278) which inundate him in his crisis.

The techniques Fitzgerald uses in the representation of events are, in one sense, as conventional as those he uses in manipulating point of view. The happenings are related chronologically, not in a tightly-knit plot sequence but, in the tradition of the saturation novel, in a series of independent scenes only loosely related. Reviewers of the book noted the lack of plot when they made such remarks as that of the reviewer for the *New York Times* – "The whole story is disconnected, more or less."[61] The reviewer for *The New Republic* referred pointedly to "the collected works of F. Scott Fitzgerald published in novel form under the title of *This Side of Paradise*."[62] In a very real sense the novel

[61] "With College Men," *The New York Times Book Review*, May 9, 1920, p. 240.
[62] R. V. A. S., "This Side of Paradise," *op. cit.*, p. 362.

was Fitzgerald's collected works. Many of the episodes and poems in the novel had been published as individual pieces before the book appeared, and they were not originally intended for the novel.[63] That they could be so readily included in the novel with little or no change suggests in itself the loose conception of the work.

But in the representation of events of *This Side of Paradise*, devices were used which made the technique seem as varied as that used in the handling of point of view: for example, the use of numerous subtitles, or "event headings," to introduce episodes not closely related to one another. These titles render unnecessary the invention of a great number of transitional elements in the text and make, therefore, for a certain economy. Since they orient the reader immediately as to the author's intent, the reader passes from episode to episode without searching for a continuous line of action or developing plot. This bold admission by Fitzgerald of the episodic nature of his novel in reality serves to maintain interest in an action generally lacking in suspense. The titles themselves are sometimes simple statements suggestive of the nature of the content, such as "Historical," (61) one paragraph informing the reader about the beginning of the war and Amory's reaction (or lack of response) to it, or such as "Descriptive," (66) a brief section devoted to a physical description of Amory at the age of eighteen. Sometimes the titles suggest a higher significance than the merely literal, such as "A Damp Symbolic Interlude," (59) and sometimes they are figurative, such as "Babes in the Woods." (73)

The representation of events in *This Side of Paradise* varies from the dramatic to the panoramic, a wide range not unusual in itself, but Fitzgerald's technical devices reach the extreme in both directions. The ultimate in panoramic representation is approached in the use of "snapshots," book lists, and letters, the ultimate in dramatic representation in the use of the actual scene, as in a drama, including, even, the stage directions. There are two such scenes in *This Side of Paradise*, the first Amory's introduction to Rosalind, the second his parting from her, both in the first chapter ("The Debutante") of Book Two.[64] As a

[63] "Babes in the Woods" (beginning on p. 73) was published as a short story in *The Smart Set*, September, 1919. "The Debutante" (beginning on p. 179) was published as a one-act play in *The Smart Set*, November, 1919. The poem, set in prose, beginning (p. 253) "When Vanity kissed Vanity..." appeared in a slightly different form in a letter to Edmund Wilson on September 26th, 1917 ("To Cecilia" in *The Crack-Up*, p. 246). The poem at the beginning of Book Two, Chapter V, appeared under the title, "The Way of Purgation," in a letter to Edmund Wilson dated Autumn of 1917 (*The Crack-Up*, p. 249).

[64] Mr. Cargill, in *Intellectual America* (p. 349), stated that Fitzgerald's method of "writing... dialogue as in a drama" was "suggested by the work of Joyce." This is

rule the dramatic manner "eliminates" the author from his work entirely; the reader is left to deduce by inference from speeches and, if there are "stage-directions," by gestures, what is transpiring in the minds of the characters. Since so much is left to inference, one of the virtues of the purely dramatic method is, presumably, its economy. On the other hand, the method makes impossible the rendering of a scene from the point of view of one of the characters; if the intellectual or otherwise internal response of one character to a situation is more significant than the objectively presented "externals" of the event itself, and if his reaction is so complex as to be incommunicable by inference, surely the dramatic method is undesirable. Fitzgerald's two episodes would seem to be excellent material for treatment in the purely dramatic manner. They are of supreme importance in the life of the protagonist but his response to them may be implied in the main by his speeches and gestures. His "delayed" reactions may be, as they are, conveyed in the more conventional narrative, related from his point of view, which follows each scene. Also the episodes are by their very nature "verbal"; an initial meeting and a final parting of "lovers." But Fitzgerald destroys some of the natural advantages of his method by resorting in the stage directions to many of the devices of conventional narrative treatment. He discusses Rosalind's past life and character: "Rosalind had been disappointed in man after man as individuals, but she had great faith in man as a sex. Women she detested." (183) And he explores her suppressed emotional reaction to the situation: "Then she turns and looks once more at the room. Here they had sat and dreamed: that tray she had so often filled with matches for him." (211) Fitzgerald thus dissipates the advantages of his method by violating the strictures which it normally imposes.

Many of the "episodes" in *This Side of Paradise*, separated from each other by the sub-titles in the book, are no more than "snapshots," or brief summaries of significant events in the life or education of the protagonist. Fitzgerald gathers several of these episodes together under the title, "Snapshots of the Young Egotist," (17) in which appear sum-

---

unlikely, for Fitzgerald first used the method in "The Debutante," published in *The Smart Set* in September, 1919, and later incorporated in *This Side of Paradise* (pp. 179 ff.). *Ulysses*, in which Joyce first used the method, was published as a book in 1922. Although it was serialized before 1922, it seems improbable that Fitzgerald had seen it before then, especially in view of his statement in a letter to Edmund Wilson dated June 29, 1922 (*The Crack-Up*, p. 26): "I have Ullysses [*sic*] from the Brick Row Bookshop & am starting it." This statement implies that Fitzgerald had not seen Joyce's novel before. Probably the method is a carry-over for Fitzgerald from the writing of dialogue and lyrics for musical comedies at Princeton.

mary accounts of Amory's experiences with his dog, of seeing a play, of his falling in love and writing a poem to the girl, of his interest in sports, of his reading, of his reaction to school, of his collecting locks of hair and rings from girls, and of his dreams and ambitions. All of this "narration" consumes less than three pages. This documentary method suits Fitzgerald's intention admirably, if his intention is to present to the fullest possible extent the influences which shaped Amory's character.

- Some years after its publication, Fitzgerald jotted down a brief description of his first book: "*This Side of Paradise:* a Romance and a Reading List."[65] It is of some interest that he should recall a device which he exploited to the fullest – the reading-list. There are five such lists in the novel,[66] besides the several more-extensive references to Amory's reading. It is possible to trace Amory's intellectual development through these book-lists. Of the very young Amory, Fitzgerald writes: "Among other things he read: 'For the Honor of the School,' 'Little Women' (twice), 'The Common Law,' 'Sapho,' 'Dangerous Dan Mcgrew,' 'The Broad Highway' (three times), 'The Fall of the House of Usher,' 'Three Weeks,' 'Mary Ware,' 'The Little Colonel's Chum,' 'Gunga Dhin,' *The Police Gazette*, and *Jim-Jam-Jems*." (18) Later reading-lists reflect Amory's maturing tastes. In a minimum of narration, these lists indicate the several stages in Amory's intellectual growth, and suggest the influences that are forming his personality. But, like many of Fitzgerald's technical devices, the reading-list has a quality of enumeration which suggests documentation.

The letters Fitzgerald uses in *This Side of Paradise* force him by their very nature to panoramic representation. Letters are "reports" of events by one character to another, and have as technical devices certain advantages. They permit the covering of much ground rapidly; they permit the revelation of certain facts or events without violation of a point of view which has been established; they inform a character (and the reader) of important facts or events which he has no logical way of learning or observing at first hand; and they may reveal a perspective on the action other than that of the fiction's primary point of view. The use of letters for panoramic representation of happenings is demonstrated fully in "Interlude," the brief section compressed between the two books of the novel. This section, covering the period from May, 1917, to February, 1919 (the war years), consists of a letter from Monsignor Darcy to Amory, a short narrative passage called

[65] F. Scott Fitzgerald, "The Notebooks," *The Crack-Up*, p. 176.
[66] Fitzgerald, *This Side of Paradise*, pp. 18, 36, 57, 116, and 224.

"Embarking at Night," and a letter from Amory to T. P. D'Invilliers. The rapidity with which a significant event may be "reported" is exemplified by Amory's almost casual remark, "Since poor Beatrice died I'll probably have a little money, but very darn little." (175) By this brief reference, the reader discovers that Amory's mother is dead. The letters permit Fitzgerald to pass over quickly a great many events in Amory's life and yet to keep his reader properly informed and adequately prepared for comprehending succeeding narration.

The fictional technique in *This Side of Paradise* is the technique of the "slice-of-life" novel. There is the representation of an abundance of events but with no apparent unifying purpose. Experiences are included because they are inherently interesting but not because they contribute to the "whole," for the "whole," except in an extremely loose sense, does not exist. The development of the theme is blurred; indeed, the theme would seem to be an accidental accretion of the several episodes rather than a dominating center toward which all of the action contributes. But Fitzgerald's techniques are remarkably varied, more so, in fact, than the material or subject would seem, ordinarily, to demand. But experimentation in technique is, perhaps, the sign of a restless and developing talent, one capable under favorable conditions of significant achievement. It would seem so, anyway, in the case of Fitzgerald.

There remains, however, something to be said for the undeniable charm of *This Side of Paradise*. Few critics have damned it without reservation. In 1922 Edmund Wilson qualified his condemnation: "I have said that 'This Side of Paradise' commits almost every sin that a novel can possibly commit; it is true that it does commit every sin except the unpardonable sin; it does not fail to live. The whole preposterous farrago is animated with life."[67] John O'Hara has recalled *This Side of Paradise* with the fond glow of remembered romance: "I cannot refrain... from comparing my first and countless subsequent meetings with that book to a first and subsequent meetings with The Girl."[68] An English critic, Alan Ross, has recently defined that element in the novel which he believes the secret of its imperfect success: "Amory Blaine, who at the end of the book cries out 'I know myself, but that is all,' fascinates, not for the superficial charm Fitzgerald endows him with, but because he, as was Fitzgerald, is himself aware of something

[67] Wilson, "The Literary Spotlight: F. Scott Fitzgerald," *op. cit.*, p. 22.
[68] John O'Hara, "Introduction," *The Portable F. Scott Fitzgerald* (New York: The Viking Press, 1945), p. vii.

beyond him, inchoate and inexpressible, that could give the lie to his whole life and conduct."[69] In spite of its faults, perhaps in part because of them, *This Side of Paradise* continues to appeal. In its very immaturity lies its charm; it is an honest and sincere book by youth about youth, containing the emotions ranging from ecstasy to despair, of the immature which the mature can neither easily recall nor evoke.

[69] Alan Ross, "Rumble Among the Drums," *Horizon*, XVIII (December, 1948), 427.

2: *THE BEAUTIFUL AND DAMNED*

A NOVEL OF TRANSITION

I. FROM MACKENZIE TO MENCKEN

In his letter to Frances Newman in February, 1921, Fitzgerald admitted that when he had begun *This Side of Paradise* his "literary taste was so unformed that Youth's Encounter was still [his] ... 'perfect book.'"[1] This remark reveals that Fitzgerald himself believed rather early that he had "outgrown" the immaturity of such literary opinions. Edmund Wilson has suggested somewhat precisely the cause and nature of the change in Fitzgerald's attitude toward the novel between *This Side of Paradise* (1920) and *The Beautiful and Damned* (1922)[2]: "Since writing 'This Side of Paradise' – on the inspiration of Wells and Mackenzie – Fitzgerald has become acquainted with another school of fiction: the ironical-pessimistic." This new "genre" in general favor, asserts Wilson, is "the kind which makes much of the tragedy and the meaninglessness of life. Hitherto, [Fitzgerald] had supposed that the thing to do was to discover a meaning in life; but he now set bravely about to produce a distressing tragedy which should be, also, 100 per cent meaningless."[3] Wilson might have added that this "school of fiction," if it was a school, had as its chief spokesmen H. L. Mencken, and that it was probably through Mencken that Fitzgerald was introduced to the new "genre."

In *The Bookman* of March, 1921, in a highly favorable review of Mencken's *Prejudices: Second Series*, Fitzgerald held that Mencken had done "more for the national letters than any man alive."[4] This extravagant praise suggests the extent of Fitzgerald's debt to Mencken during this period. There exists additional evidence of Fitzgerald's high regard. In a speech before the Women's City Club in St. Paul late in 1921, recorded by Thomas A. Boyd, Fitzgerald praised Mencken in much the same terms as in his review: "'Before I return to my subject I want to take a few minutes to talk about a man who has, I believe, done more for contemporary American literature than any other man alive. His name is H. L. Mencken' (Reads a few lines from Mr. Men-

---

[1] Newman, *op. cit.*, p. 41.

[2] *The Beautiful and Damned* was serialized in *The Metropolitan Magazine* from September, 1921, to March, 1922. Fitzgerald was still revising his novel, however, after it began appearing as a serial. On November 25, 1921, he wrote to Edmund Wilson (*The Crack-Up*, p. 256): "I have almost completely rewritten my book."

[3] Wilson, "The Literary Spotlight: F. Scott Fitzgerald," *op. cit.*, pp. 23–24.

[4] Fitzgerald, "The Baltimore Anti-Christ," *The Bookman*, LIII (March, 1921), 81.

cken to prove it.)"[5] In an interview with Boyd, which took place in August, 1921, Fitzgerald stated that he knew nothing about Mencken before *This Side of Paradise* was written. In reply to Boyd's assertion that he thought he saw "a Baltimore forefinger in This Side of Paradise," Fitzgerald somewhat surprisingly answered: "'Well! I don't think Main Street would have been written if Mencken hadn't been born. ... but that isn't true with This Side of Paradise. It was not until after I had got the proofs of my book back from the publishers that I learned of Mencken. I happened across the Smart Set one day and I thought 'Here's a man whose name I ought to know. I guess I'll stick it in the proof sheets.' But I've met Mencken since then and I'm glad I put his name in.'"[6] The fact that Fitzgerald had published a short story in *The Smart Set* in September, 1919, seems to have slipped his mind, but we can agree with him that his genuine acquaintance with Mencken did not begin until after *This Side of Paradise*.

"The National Letters," the first essay in *Prejudices: Second Series* (the book that Fitzgerald reviewed so favorably) sets forth the basic ideas and attitudes which run through *The Beautiful and Damned*. Since in his second novel Fitzgerald was apparently trying to write what Mencken called "superior fiction,"[7] it is of interest to examine just what Mencken considered the components of such writing. Mencken's discussion of "the fundamental defects of American fiction" incidentally revealed what he thought to be the mark of great writing. American fiction, Mencken said, "habitually exhibits, not a man of delicate organization in revolt against the inexplicable tragedy of existence, but a man of low sensibilities and elemental desires yielding himself gladly to his environment." The quality of fiction is determined not by the artistry of the novelist but by the attitude and character of the protagonist. The general run of mediocre fiction, thought Mencken, appealed to base and ignoble interests: "The man of reflective habit cannot conceivably take any passionate interest in the conflicts it [American popular fiction] deals with. He doesn't want to marry the daughter of the owner of the hook-and-eye factory; he would probably burn down the factory itself if it ever came into his hands." This rare man is passionately interested in the "far more poignant and significant conflict between a salient individual and the harsh and meaningless fiats of destiny, the

[5] Thomas A. Boyd, "Scott Fitzgerald Speaks at Home," *St. Paul Daily News*, December 4, 1921.

[6] Thomas A. Boyd, "Literary Libels: Francis Scott Key Fitzgerald," *St. Paul Daily News*, March 5, 1922.

[7] H. L. Mencken. *Prejudices: Second Series* (New York: Alfred A. Knopf, 1920), p. 41.

unintelligible mandates and vagaries of God. His hero is not one who yields and wins, but one who resists and fails."[8] As Fitzgerald was to realize later, Mencken's "idea" of literature was "ethical rather than aesthetic."[9] All superior literature must, he thought, reflect a prescribed "tragic" attitude toward life.

Since this philosophical attitude (belief that the "fiats of destiny" are meaningless and the "mandates and vagaries of God" are unintelligible) results in an inner struggle which, "nine times out of ten," ends in failure in real life, "the theme of the great bulk of superior fiction," Mencken concluded, is "character in decay." In this general tragic view Mencken found the common meeting ground of Dostoievsky, Balzac, Hardy, Conrad, Flaubert, Zola, Turgenieff, Goethe, Sudermann, Bennett, and Dreiser. "In nearly all first-rate novels the hero is defeated. In perhaps a majority he is completely destroyed."[10] In America, "the national fear of ideas, the democratic distrust of whatever strikes beneath the prevailing platitudes" caused the literature to evade dealing with "what, after all, must be every healthy literature's elementary materials."[11] In *The Beautiful and Damned*, Fitzgerald's major theme, as Edmund Wilson indicated, is the meaninglessness of life. The story shows, or was meant to show, the "decay" of his hero, Anthony Patch: "a man of delicate organization in revolt against the inexplicable tragedy of existence."

In attacking what he called "the literature of Greenwich Village," Mencken commented, "What commonly engulfs and spoils the Villagers is their concern with mere technique.... Half the wars in the Village are over form; content is taken for granted, or forgotten altogether." This "concentration upon externals" Mencken considered "childish."[12] Mencken's lack of respect for the importance of fictional technique enabled him to place Dreiser indiscriminately in the same group with Conrad; Mencken could, perhaps, separate the superior writers from the inferior, but his theory of the novel did not enable him to make more complex and more subtle, but no less vital distinctions. Still if, through him, Fitzgerald's taste for such writers as Robert W. Chambers and Robert H. Benson was destroyed, and his interest in such novelists as Dreiser and Conrad was stimulated, Mencken performed good service in Fitzgerald's artistic development.

Fitzgerald's book reviews of this period (1921) indicate the extent

---

[8] *Ibid.*, pp. 39–41.
[9] Fitzgerald, "How to Waste Material," *The Bookman*, LXIII (May, 1926), 263.
[10] *Ibid.*, p. 41.
[11] *Ibid.*, p. 16.
[12] *Ibid.*, pp. 25–29.

of his development under the tutelage of Mencken. In September, 1921, his review of John Dos Passos's *Three Soldiers* showed that he was most impressed by the book's attitude, which would "frighten the caravanseries of one hundred and twenty-proof Americans, dollar a year men and slaughter crazy old maids.... The whole gorgeous farce of 1917–1918 will be laid before [the readers]." Although Fitzgerald saw the merit of the novel primarily in its attitude, he did devote one brief comment to technique: "There is none of that uncorrelated detail, that clumsy juggling with huge masses of material which shows in all but one or two pieces of American realism. The author is not oppressed by the panicstricken necessity of using all his data at once lest some other prophet of the new revelation uses it before him. He is an artist – John Dos Passos."[13] Although these remarks are inadequate, even in a brief review, for the experimental technique of *Three Soldiers*, they show a growing awareness on Fitzgerald's part of the importance of method. His notation that there was no "uncorrelated detail" in the novel suggests that he had moved some distance from the tradition of the saturation novel. And it is of some significance that Fitzgerald underlined his praise of the technique by calling Dos Passos "an artist." Fitzgerald had, perhaps, begun to realize that the technique of the novel is but another term for the art of the novel.

In his review of Charles G. Norris's *Brass* (November, 1921), Fitzgerald remembered his ignorance of Zola, Frank Norris, Dreiser and other realists until "Brigadier General Mencken... marshaled the critics in quiescent column of squads for the campaign against Philistia." *Brass*, however, did not seem to Fitzgerald a good novel: "Although it is a more difficult form than Salt and is just as well, perhaps more gracefully constructed, the parallel marriages are by no means so deftly handled as the ones in Arnold Bennett's 'Whom God Hath Joined.'... It is a cold book throughout and it left me unmoved. Mr. Norris has an inexhaustible theme and he elaborates on it intelligently and painstakingly – but, it seems to me, without passion and without pain."[14] The observation concerning the construction of *Brass* suggests an interest in form, but is so phrased as to imply that form is only of secondary importance. Since emphasis is placed on *Brass's* being a "cold book throughout," the primary flaw appears to be the book's lack of "passion." If by passion Fitzgerald meant the emotion of the author expended on his theme or action, then perhaps "passion" is in conflict

[13] Fitzgerald, "Three Soldiers," *St. Paul Daily News*, September 25, 1921. Not only Mencken's ideas but also the Menckenesque style here is striking.
[14] Fitzgerald, "Poor Old Marriage," *The Bookman*, LIV (November, 1921), 253.

with form. One of Henry James's major objections to the saturation novelists was that they let an "affirmation of energy... constitute for them the treatment of a theme." James would have agreed that only when an author is able to view his experience (out of which he derives his material) dispassionately and objectively can he begin to give it shape and coherence in the form of art.

In the conclusion of his review of *Brass* Fitzgerald referred to his changing personal taste in the novel: "A novel interests me on one of two counts: either it is something entirely new and fresh and profoundly felt, as for instance, 'The Red Badge of Courage' or 'Salt,' or else it is a tour de force by a man of exceptional talent, a Mark Twain or a Tarkington. A great book is both of these things."[15] At about this same time (November, 1921) Fitzgerald confessed to Edmund Wilson, "I am tired of modern novels."[16] Perhaps his waning interest in the new novels was a sign of a maturing taste. Certainly Fitzgerald had advanced from his former indiscriminate enthusiasm for practically everything he read, good and bad. His very attempt to define a "great book" (perhaps the influence of H. L. Mencken) demonstrates that he had departed from the tradition of the saturation novel and was groping about for a new set of criteria under which to develop as a novelist. In the evolution of his fictional technique he was somewhere midpoint between the novel of saturation and the novel of selection – in a period of transition.

II. FLAPPERS, PHILOSOPHERS, AND THE JAZZ AGE

Fitzgerald's short stories do not fit precisely into a history of the development of his fictional technique in the novel. One cause probably lies in the basic difference between the two art forms: the length of the short story arbitrarily imposes on it some sort of unity even though of a superficial kind. Not even Wells argued for *irrelevance* in the short story: in the same essay in which he defended the right of the novel to abound in irrelevancies, he excepted the short story: "Edgar Allan Poe was very definite upon the point that the short story should be finished at a sitting. But the novel and the short story are two entirely different things, and the train of reasoning that made the American master limit the short story to about an hour of reading as a maximum, does not apply to the longer work." Wells modeled his concept of the short story on principles enunciated by Poe: "A short story is, or should be, a simple

---

[15] *Ibid.*, p. 254.
[16] Fitzgerald, "Letters to Friends," *The Crack-Up*, p. 256.

thing; it aims at producing one single, vivid effect; it has to seize the attention at the outset, and never relaxing, gather it together more and more until the climax is reached. The limits of the human capacity to attend closely therefore set a limit to it; it must explode and finish before interruption occurs or fatigue sets in."[17] Whether or not Wells's concept of the short story influenced Fitzgerald, Fitzgerald's short fiction, even that written for the popular magazines, shows more form and unity than his early novels.

Another difficulty of fitting Fitzgerald's short stories into an account of his development as an artist is that he admittedly wrote them on two levels. When Margaret Anderson, out scouting for material for her *Little Review*, met Fitzgerald in Scribner's looking over the proofs for *This Side of Paradise*, he "regretted with blushes that his stuff was too popular to be solicited by a magazine of the new prose." When she saw him two years later, "he was still blushing because he was receiving checks from Harper's Bazaar."[18] Fitzgerald had every right to be ashamed of much of the short fiction he was writing; but at least his blushes suggest that he did not try to deceive himself about the quality of the stories that he wrote to sell to the popular magazines. In 1920 he informed Edmund Wilson, "Have sold three or four cheap stories to American magazines"; in November, 1921, he wrote again, "Have written two good short stories and three cheap ones." In January, 1922, he reported to Wilson the results of his attempt to sell what he considered to be his best fiction: "I have written two wonderful stories & get letters of praise from six editors with the addenda that 'our readers, however, would be offended.' Very discouraging."[19]

Between the publication of *This Side of Paradise* and the appearance of *The Beautiful and Damned*, Fitzgerald wrote and published a large number of short stories, most of which were collected and published in two volumes; *Flappers and Philosophers* (September, 1920) and *Tales of the Jazz Age* (September, 1922). None of the stories of the first volume is of particular interest in a study of the development of Fitzgerald's fictional technique, although many of them, such as "The Offshore Pirate," could be used to document the fact — were further documentation necessary — that Fitzgerald was investing his characters and settings with a glamour which they did not deserve. Probably the secret of the popular success of his stories is that they served as escape

[17] Wells, "The Contemporary Novel," *op. cit.*, pp. 862–63.

[18] Margaret Anderson, *My Thirty Years' War* (New York: Corici, Friede Publishers, 1930), pp. 43–44.

[19] Fitzgerald, "Letters to Friends," *The Crack-Up*, pp. 254–57.

for all the bored five-and-ten clerks who dreamed of being glamorous Fitzgerald flappers courted lavishly by disguised millionaire philosophers.

Fitzgerald wrote in the table of contents of his second volume of short stories, "I tender these tales of the Jazz Age into the hands of those who read as they run and run as they read." Fitzgerald's comments on a number of his stories in this unusual table of contents indicate that he took some of his stories as lightly as this flippant remark suggests. "The Camel's Back," he said, "was written during one day in the city of New Orleans, with the express purpose of buying a platinum and diamond wrist watch which cost six hundred dollars."[20] Without this confession, it is difficult enough to take "The Camel's Back," with its trite plot and mediocre execution, as the work of a serious writer; in the face of Fitzgerald's remark, it is impossible not to become irritated at his flagrant and even defiant waste of talent.

Fitzgerald's frivolous, perhaps even irresponsible, attitude toward his work is exhibited also in his comment on "Mr. Icky": "This has the distinction of being the only magazine piece ever written in a New York hotel. The business was done in a bedroom in the Knickerbocker, and shortly afterward that memorable hostelry closed its doors forever." On occasion Fitzgerald's commentary frankly reveals the defects in his stories which he recognized in the writing but simply did not bother to correct. When he wrote "O Russet Witch!" he had just completed the first draft of *The Beautiful and Damned* and, he said, a "natural reaction" made him "revel in a story wherein none of the characters need be taken seriously.... I'm afraid that I was somewhat carried away by the feeling that there was no ordered scheme to which I must conform."[21]

But Fitzgerald's low estimate of a number of his stories causes those which he considered as serious efforts to stand out sharply in contrast, sometimes embarrassingly so. Fitzgerald commented on "The Lees of Happiness": "Of this story I can say that it came to me in an irresistible form, crying to be written. It will be accused perhaps of being a mere piece of sentimentality, but, as I saw it, it was a great deal more. If, therefore, it lacks the ring of sincerity, or even of tragedy, the fault rests not with the theme but with my handling of it."[22] Fitzgerald must have realized that he had missed the effect for which he had striven in

[20] F. Scott Fitzgerald, *Tales of the Jazz Age* (New York: Charles Scribner's Sons, 1922), pp. viii–xi.

[21] *Ibid.*, pp. ix–x.

[22] *Ibid.*

the story; his comment indicates that he was aware that the failure lay not in his material but in his technique. Fitzgerald's quick awareness and frequently clear understanding of his own failure in craftsmanship must have figured importantly in the development of his fictional technique.

There are two stories in *Tales of the Jazz Age* that deserve a close examination in this study – "May Day," the longest of all Fitzgerald's short stories, and "The Diamond as Big as the Ritz," one of the most frequently anthologized. "May Day," first published in *The Smart Set* in July, 1920, is of interest primarily because of the unusual technique employed in it. In the table of contents Fitzgerald revealed the source of his material and the theme which he attempted to impose upon it in "May Day": "This somewhat unpleasant tale... relates a series of events which took place in the spring of [1919].... Each of the three events made a great impression upon me. In life they were unrelated, except by the general hysteria of that spring which inaugurated the Age of Jazz, but in my story I have tried, unsuccessfully I fear, to weave them into a pattern – a pattern which would give the effect of those months in New York as they appeared to at least one member of what was then the younger generation."[23] Fitzgerald's material was, obviously, rather unwieldy and difficult to shape into any kind of unified or coherent pattern. If as he says he wished to evoke the general hysteria of postwar New York in 1919, the "spring which inaugurated the Age of Jazz," the technique which he evolved for the task seems admirably suited to do such a theme justice. It is the technique which John Dos Passos was to use later on a much larger scale: the independent and simultaneous development of several apparently unrelated lines of action which are merged occasionally in seemingly accidental ways. All of the lines of action, though only loosely related to each other in plot, are directly and intimately associated in theme, and any occasional "contacts" serve a thematic purpose.

The primary advantage of such a technique is that it allows for the development of "large" themes on several levels – themes which involve (as does the theme in "May Day") such complex intangibles as the "mood" or "atmosphere" of a nation. But there is a disadvantage to the technique which would increase in direct ratio to the length of a work: the lack of a single line of continuous action to sustain the reader's interest through a heightening suspense. In such a technique, theme becomes more significant than plot or story and must therefore fulfill *their* function by absorbing the interest of the reader. In comparatively

[23] *Ibid.*, p. viii.

short works, this burden does not seem to be too heavy for the theme, but in longer works the danger of the lapse of the interest of the reader would appear to be great. If John Dos Passos has succeeded with the method in comparatively long works, it is because he has overcome its handicap by using it skillfully and in conjunction with other techniques. Called a novelette in *The Smart Set*, "May Day" covers some sixty-six pages in *Tales of the Jazz Age*. Something longer than a short story, something shorter than a novel, its size is, perhaps, ideal for such a technique because it is long enough to allow for the adequate development of several independent lines of action, and, at the same time, it is not so long that it tends to confuse the reader by its diversity or to lose his interest by its lack of narrative suspense.

In the first few paragraphs of "May Day," Fitzgerald prepares the reader for his special method by an unusual device: he devotes five introductory paragraphs to the "setting," or the time and place of his story – without actually revealing either. This opening passage serves not only expository but also thematic purposes:

> There had been a war fought and won and the great city of the conquering people was crossed with triumphal arches and vivid with thrown flowers of white, red, and rose. All through the long spring days the returning soldiers marched up the chief highway behind the strump of drums and joyous, resonant wind of the brasses, while merchants and clerks left their bickerings and figurings and, crowding to the windows, turned their white-bunched faces gravely upon the passing battalions.
>
> Never had there been such splendor in the great city, for the victorious war had brought plenty in its train, and the merchants had flocked thither from the South and West with their households to taste of all the luscious feasts and witness the lavish entertainments prepared – and to buy for their women furs against the next winter and bags of golden mesh and varicolored slippers of silk and silver and rose satin and cloth of gold.
>
> So gaily and noisily were the peace and prosperity impending hymned by the scribes and poets of the conquering people that more and more spenders had gathered from the provinces to drink the wine of excitement, and faster and faster did the merchants dispose of their trinkets and slippers until they sent up a mighty cry for more trinkets and more slippers in order that they might give in barter what was demanded of them. Some even of them flung up their hands helplessly, shouting:
>
> "Alas! I have no more slippers! and alas! I have no more trinkets! May Heaven help me, for I know not what I shall do!"
>
> But no one listened to their great outcry, for the throngs were far too busy – day by day, the foot-soldiers trod jauntily the highway and all exulted because the young men returning were

pure and brave, sound of tooth and pink of cheek, and the young
women of the land were virgins and comely both of face and of
figure.
   So during all this time there were many adventures that happened in the great city, and, of these, several – or perhaps one – are
here set down.[24]

By the use of biblical diction and phraseology and by withholding the
specific time and the specific names of the place and the people, Fitzgerald suggests the universality of his theme – the general hysteria and
confusion of values which follow war. After this preparation for the
overriding significance of theme and for the general nature of the
events and characters in the story to follow, Fitzgerald reveals the
technique which he has used: the several "adventures" which are "here
set down" are "perhaps one" in the sense that they all merge into one
theme.
   Evidently Fitzgerald used no model for the technique in "May Day."
His commentary implies that he invented the method for his own purposes in this one story. Although he never resorted to the technique
again, his experimentation with it in "May Day" suggests his growing
concern for finding the right technique for a particular subject and
marks an important advance in his attitude toward his art.
   "The Diamond as Big as the Ritz" first appeared in *The Smart Set* in
June, 1922, and was later placed in the group of stories in *Tales of the
Jazz Age* which Fitzgerald labeled "Fantasies." Fitzgerald commented
on this group:

> These next stories are written in what, were I of imposing stature,
> I should call my "second manner." "The Diamond as Big as the
> Ritz," which appeared last summer in the "Smart Set," was
> designed utterly for my own amusement. I was in that familiar
> mood characterized by a perfect craving for luxury, and the story
> began as an attempt to feed that craving on imaginary foods.
> One well-known critic has been pleased to like this extravaganza
> better than anything I have written. Personally I prefer "The Off
> Shore Pirate." But, to tamper slightly with Lincoln: If you like
> this sort of thing, this, possibly, is the sort of thing you'll like.[25]

From these remarks one might gather that Fitzgerald did not take his
story seriously. When he said, however, that he "began [the story] as an
attempt to feed that craving [for luxury] on imaginary foods," perhaps
he was implying that it *grew* into something more significant. In a letter
to Edmund Wilson in June, 1922, he asked, "Did you like *The Diamond*

[24] *Ibid.*, pp. 61–62.
[25] *Ibid.*, p. viii.

as Big as the Ritz or did you read it. It's in my new book any how."[26]
His singling out this one story for inquiry suggests that he regarded it as
a greater achievement than his somewhat nonchalant remarks imply.

"The Diamond as Big as the Ritz" is Fitzgerald's first treatment of a
theme stressing the core of corruption deep within limitless and fabulous
riches, the simultaneous attraction and repulsion of great wealth. It is
interesting that Fitzgerald cast his first treatment of this theme in the
form of a fantasy, in which the symbolism was an integral part of the
story. When he returned to the theme later, in "realistic" tales, the
symbolism was perhaps a carry-over from his experimental fantasies.
In "The Diamond as Big as the Ritz" Fitzgerald discovered a method
to extend meaning, to universalize experience, and this story represents
a step further toward the novel of selection.

The story is related through the consciousness of John. T. Unger,
beginning with his growing awe of the wealth which he sees at the
fabulous Washington estate built on a diamond mountain in Montana
and ending with the horror in his gradual realization of the terrifying
cruelty and polluted morality which the wealth conceals and on which
it rests. Fitzgerald's description of John Unger's first evening at the
Washington home is one of the story's finest touches:

> Afterward John remembered that first night as a daze of many
> colors, of quick sensory impressions, of music soft as a voice in love,
> and of the beauty of things, lights and shadows, and motions and
> faces. There was a whitehaired man who stood drinking a many-
> hued cordial from a crystal thimble set on a golden stem. There
> was a girl with a flowery face, dressed like Titania with braided
> sapphires in her hair. There was a room where the solid, soft gold
> of the walls yielded to the pressure of his hand, and a room that
> was like a platonic conception of the ultimate prison – ceiling,
> floor, and all, it was lined with an unbroken mass of diamonds,
> diamonds of every size and shape, until, lit with tall violet lamps
> in the corners, it dazzled the eyes with a whiteness that could be
> compared only with itself, beyond human wish or dream.[27]

By describing the evening as John remembers it in retrospect, Fitzgerald is able to *select* only those details of John's experience which
glitter and dazzle still in his memory; in one compact paragraph Fitzgerald conveys the overwhelming impression which the fabulous riches
made on John.

Fitzgerald's symbolism seems to function most effectively in the final
scene, after the Washington estate has been bombed and Braddock

---

[26] Fitzgerald, "Letters to Friends," *The Crack-Up*, p. 260.
[27] Fitzgerald, *Tales of the Jazz Age*, p. 151.

Washington resorts to a final fantastic effort to save his diamond mountain. John, searching a means of escape from the debacle, becomes suddenly aware of Washington standing on a ledge of his diamond mountain, "silhouetted against the gray sky." Unger thinks at first that Washington is praying, but "there... [is] something in the man's whole attitude antithetical to prayer." There is "a quality of monstrous condescension" in his voice when he speaks: "Oh, you above there!" Two slaves stand behind him staggering beneath the weight of an enormous, "exquisitely chiselled diamond." Puzzled at first by this incongruous scene, John suddenly realizes that he is witnessing Braddock Washington "offering a bribe to God!" The diamond held by the slaves is but "a promise of more to follow," as Washington promises God "the greatest diamond in the world":

> This diamond would be cut with many more thousand facets than there were leaves on a tree, and yet the whole diamond would be shaped with the perfection of a stone no bigger than a fly. Many men would work upon it for many years. It would be set in a great dome of beaten gold, wonderfully carved and equipped with gates of opal and crusted sapphire. In the middle would be hollowed out a chapel presided over by an altar of iridescent, decomposing, ever-changing radium which would burn out the eyes of any worshipper who lifted up his head from prayer – and on this altar there would be slain for the amusement of the Divine Benefactor any victim He should choose, even though it should be the greatest and most powerful man alive.

Braddock Washington "doubted only whether he had made his bribe big enough. God had His price, of course." But as John stares in "giddy fascination" at this scene, a "curious phenomenon" occurs: "It was as though the sky had darkened for an instant, as though there had been a sudden murmur in a gust of wind, a sound of far-away trumpets, a sighing like the rustle of a great silken robe – for a time the whole of nature round about partook of this darkness; the birds' song ceased; the trees were still, and far over the mountain there was a mutter of dull, menacing thunder.... God had refused to accept the bribe."[28] That wealth, so appealing and dazzling at first, reveals the boundless extent of its corruption in the incalculable insolence of its attempt to bribe Creation. The horror behind the glitter does indeed emerge as John T. Unger looks directly into the corrupt heart of great riches – riches which have been created by a brutal disregard for human – or divine – beings.

[28] *Ibid.*, pp. 183–86.

"May Day" and "The Diamond as Big as the Ritz" mark important steps in the development of Fitzgerald's fictional technique. In the one he showed a growing consciousness of the importance of technique to theme; in the other he discovered the possibilities of symbolism in conveying complex meaning. These two stories stand as testimony that Fitzgerald was not dissipating his talent completely in writing for the popular magazines. In some of his short fiction, he was using experimental techniques, and these experiments, besides having interest in their own right, were to prove valuable to him in his longer works. But the difference between the short story and the novel is deceptively simple; the leap from skill in the one to skill in the other is not so simple, or at least does not seem so in Fitzgerald's case. His next novel, *The Beautiful and Damned*, although an advance technically over *This Side of Paradise*, did not show the virtuosity in technique of the short stories.

III. THE MEANINGLESSNESS OF LIFE

The Beautiful and Damned, serialized in *The Metropolitan Magazine* from September, 1921, to March, 1922, and published as a book in 1922, is the story of the deterioration (or, to use Mencken's word, "decay") of Anthony Patch, who, while waiting to inherit his grandfather's millions, leads an idle and purposeless life of dissipation and debauchery, and of his wife, Gloria Gilbert, a superficially sophisticated girl whose only virtue is her great beauty. Their disintegration is accelerated when Grandfather Patch, a great "reformer," stumbles accidentally into one of their wild parties and, horrified by their "sin," cuts them out of his will. After a long drawn-out lawsuit contesting the will, Anthony and Gloria finally win thirty million dollars. When last seen, Anthony is apparently broken both physically and mentally, and Gloria's beauty is gradually fading.

One reviewer thought that *The Beautiful and Damned* was a "document... of distraught and abandoned but intensely living youth."[29] Another stated: "It is a tragedy, the tragedy of a poor-spirited, worthless, badly educated and over-sophisticated man, and of his wife, a selfish, spoiled and irresolute girl of great beauty of face and none of soul."[30] One critic asserted that "to the reader he [Anthony Patch] never seems one-third as intelligent as the author apparently thinks him."[31]

[29] Henry Seidel Canby, "The Flapper's Tragedy," *The Literary Review of the New York Evening Post*, II (March 4, 1922), 463.
[30] "A Dance of the Midges," *The Literary Digest*, LXXIV (July 15, 1922), 53.
[31] Louise Maunsell Field, "The Beautiful and Damned," *The New York Times Book Review*, March 5, 1922, p. 16.

These judgments suggest the ambiguity of the moral position of Fitzgerald's leading characters: it was difficult to know whether Fitzgerald
wanted to evoke sympathy or disapproval for Anthony and Gloria.
Although there was some confusion among the reviewers concerning
Fitzgerald's moral judgment of his characters, there was no lack of
agreement that his novel suffered from a deficiency of direction or
purpose. As one reviewer put it, "This [banality and commonplaceness]
comes, possibly, from a refusal to subject his spontaneous outbursts to
the refining process of self-criticism and to the clarification of a plan."[32]

In his reply to a letter from John Peale Bishop inquiring as to what
aspects of *The Beautiful and Damned* Fitzgerald would like discussed in
a book review, Fitzgerald suggested that Bishop write about the characters, "exactly whether they are good or bad, convincing or not";
about the style, whether it is "too ornate (if so quote) good (also quote)";
about the ideas: "If [they]... are bogus hold them up specifically and
laugh at them"; about "what emotion (if any) the book gave"; and
about whether the novel maintains interest: "How interesting. What
recent American books are more so." These remarks probably reveal
Fitzgerald's primary anxieties about his book and, incidentally, imply
much as to his esthetic concept of the novel at this time. Near the end
of this letter to Bishop, Fitzgerald confirmed the general charge of the
reviewers: "I'm so afraid of all the reviews being general and I devoted
so much more care myself to the *detail* of the book than I did to thinking
out the *general* scheme that I would appreciate a detailed review."[33]
Fitzgerald's admission in this casual remark seems corroborated by
Thomas Boyd's description, based on a personal interview in 1922, of
Fitzgerald's writing habits: "His [Fitzgerald's] writing is never thought
out. He creates his characters and they are likely to lead him into almost
any situation. His phrasing is done in the same way. It is rare that he
searches for a word. Most of the time words come to his mind and they
spill themselves in a riotous frenzy of song and color all over the page.
Some days he writes as many as 7,000 or 8,000 words; and then, with
a small Roget's Thesaurus, he carefully goes over his work, substituting
synonyms for any unusual words that appear more than once in seven
or eight consecutive pages."[34]

It is difficult to determine just what *The Beautiful and Damned* is *about*,
what its "general scheme," which Fitzgerald admittedly neglected, is

[32] Burton Rascoe, "Novels from the Younger Men," *The Bookman*, LV (May, 1922),
305.
[33] Fitzgerald, "Letters to Friends," *The Crack-Up*, p. 258.
[34] Thomas A. Boyd, "Literary Libels: Francis Scott Key Fitzgerald," *op. cit.*

(if, indeed, it exists). Fitzgerald, in his interview with Thomas Boyd, said casually of *The Beautiful and Damned*, "It's something after the manner of Linda Condon. Hergesheimer tried to show the effect on a woman after her once legitimate beauty had passed. That is what I am trying to do with Gloria."[35] If one can believe the sub-title in each issue of *The Metropolitan Magazine* in which the work first appeared, it is "A Searching Novel of the Revolt of American Youth." Although it is doubtful that this phrase is Fitzgerald's, *revolt*, certainly, is an important element in the novel. And in *The Beautiful and Damned* there is (as there was not in *This Side of Paradise*) a character in the central action who embodies all of those conventions which are rebelled *against*. Adam Patch is Victorianism personified:

> ... after a severe attack of sclerosis, he determined to consecrate the remainder of his life to the moral regeneration of the world. He became a reformer among reformers. Emulating the magnificent efforts of Anthony Comstock, after whom his grandson was named, he levelled a varied assortment of uppercuts and body-blows at liquor, literature, vice, art, patent medicines, and Sunday theatres. His mind, under the influence of that insidious mildew which eventually forms on all but the few, gave itself up furiously to every indignation of the age. From an armchair in the office of his Tarrytown estate he directed against the enormous hypothetical enemy, unrighteousness, a campaign which went on through fifteen years, during which he displayed himself a rabid monomaniac, an unqualified nuisance, and an intolerable bore. (4)[36]

A large part of *The Beautiful and Damned* is concerned with Anthony and Gloria's rejection of the kind of life Grandfather Patch symbolizes. Were this rebellion central throughout, the theme would be simply a definite statement of that revolt which was but a "gesture" in *This Side of Paradise*.

But the theme in *The Beautiful and Damned* is not just an extension and clarification of the theme in *This Side of Paradise*. Edmund Wilson defined the essential difference between the two books when he said that Fitzgerald, in his first novel, "supposed that the thing to do was to discover a meaning in life," while in his second, he made "much of the tragedy and 'the meaninglessness of life.'"[37] In the *Beautiful and Damned*, Anthony Patch justifies his way of living, his doing nothing, by his philosophy of "The Meaninglessness of Life." (54) His friend,

[35] *Ibid.*

[36] Quotations from *The Beautiful and Damned* (New York: Charles Scribner's Sons, 1922) are located in the text by page number in parentheses.

[37] Wilson, "The Literary Spotlight: F. Scott Fitzgerald," *op. cit.*, p. 24.

Maury Noble, although he, too, believes life meaningless, proposes a cynical compromise of working in order "to become immensely rich as quickly as possible." (43) Dick Caramel, the third of a trio clearly meant to symbolize three different attitudes, believes that life has meaning and dimly thinks that he is "contributing" by his mediocre talent as a writer. The attitudes which these characters represent emerge clearly in a short conversation which interrupts Maury Noble's monologue in the midnight symposium scene, Book II, Chapter II:

> "There's only one lesson to be learned from life, any way," interrupted Gloria, not in contradiction but in a sort of melancholy agreement.
> "What's that?" demanded Maury sharply.
> "That there's no lesson to be learned from life."
> After a short silence Maury said:
> "Young Gloria, the beautiful and merciless lady, first looked at the world with the fundamental sophistication I have struggled to attain, that Anthony never will attain, that Dick will never fully understand." (255)

This "fundamental sophistication" with which Gloria was born and for which the others struggle is the instinctive understanding of the total lack of meaning in life and the consequential refusal to acknowledge the existence of valid standards or values.

There seem to be, then, two themes in *The Beautiful and Damned*, one concerned with the revolt of youth and the other with the meaninglessness of life, both developed side by side but never quite merging into a unified view. As one reviewer said, "Fitzgerald no more believes that life is meaningless than he believes in prohibition. Yet his novel 'The Beautiful and Damned' could be interpreted either as a variation on the now popular futility theme, or a tract to back up the slogan of the Women's Christian Temperance Union."[38] If Fitzgerald wished to treat the theme of revolt sympathetically, presumably he wanted the reader not only to disapprove what was being revolted *against*, but also to see some positive justification for the rebels. By making life "meaningless," he has succeeded in depriving the revolt of significance. The characters, who, at the same time that they are embodiments of the revolt, also represent sophisticated philosophies of the meaninglessness of life, puzzle and dismay the reader by their simultaneous attraction and repulsion.

There is some indication that Fitzgerald himself was not certain of

[38] Woodward Boyd, "The Fitzgerald Legend," *St. Paul Daily News*, December 10, 1922.

his attitude toward his two leading characters. Two significant paragraphs concluded the story in the magazine version but were deleted from the book:

> That exquisite heavenly irony which has tabulated the demise of many generations of sparrows seems to us to be content with the moral judgments of man upon fellow man. If there is a subtle and yet more nebulous ethic somewhere in the mind, one might believe that beneath the sordid dress and near the bruised heart of this transaction there was a motive which was not weak but only futile and sad. In the search for happiness, which search is the greatest and possibly the only crime of which we in our petty misery are capable, these two people were marked as guilty chiefly by the freshness and fullness of their desire. Their disillusion was always a comparative thing — they had sought glamor and color through their respective worlds with steadfast loyalty — sought it and it alone in kisses and in wine, sought it with the same ingenuousness in the wanton moonlight as under the cold sun of inviolate chastity. Their fault was not that they had doubted but that they had believed.
>
> The exquisite perfection of their boredom, the delicacy of their inattention, the inexhaustibility of their discontent — were disastrous extremes — that was all. And if, before Gloria yielded up her gift of beauty, she shed one bright feather of light so that someone, gazing up from the grey earth, might say, "Look! There is an angel's wing!" perhaps she had given more than enough for her tinsel joys.[39]

Perhaps Fitzgerald omitted this passage from the book version of his novel because he realized the technical crudity of his stepping forth at the end of his story to "moralize," no matter how poetically, about his characters. He seems, throughout the passage, to be defending and justifying them, attempting to evoke a last-minute sympathy for them. Perhaps he came to realize that Anthony and Gloria did not emerge with the fresh charm he had originally conceived as theirs, and that this failure tended to invalidate his theme.

This discarded passage reveals that Fitzgerald, at the time of writing *The Beautiful and Damned*, was still too close to his material to see it clearly, too much enchanted by the outward glitter of his own creation to perceive its inner falseness. Instead of childish nonsense, he apparently found mature sophistication in "the exquisite perfection of their [Anthony and Gloria's] boredom, the delicacy of their inattention, the inexhaustibility of their discontent." It requires more than Gloria's "gift of beauty" for the reader, "gazing up from the grey earth," to see

[39] F. Scott Fitzgerald, "The Beautiful and Damned," *The Metropolitan Magazine*, LV (March, 1922), 113.

the value in her that Fitzgerald saw. Her "fundamental sophistication" turns out too often to be nothing more than an immature and sometimes painful snobbishness. At one point in her "exquisite" boredom she cries out: "Millions of people swarming like rats, chattering like apes, smelling like all hell... monkeys! Or lice, I suppose. For one really exquisite palace... on Long Island, say – or even in Greenwich ... for one palace full of pictures from the Old World and exquisite things – with avenues of trees and green lawns and a view of the blue sea, and lovely people about in slick dresses... I'd sacrifice a hundred thousand of them, a million of them." (394) Fitzgerald might plead for understanding of Anthony and Gloria, but their actions echo far louder than his words in the reader's mind. He cannot invalidate that action, as he seems to have attempted in these discarded closing paragraphs, by author's special dispensation.

When Fitzgerald says in defense of Anthony and Gloria that the search for happiness "is the greatest and possibly the only crime of which we in our petty misery are capable," he reveals not only their "philosophy" but also his own attitude. Just how fully he was in agreement with the views of his characters is suggested in a letter to Edmund Wilson (November, 1921): "Do you remember you told me that in my midnight symposium scene I had sort of set the stage for a play that never came off – in other words when they all began to talk none of them had anything important to say. I've interpolated some recent ideas of my own and (possibly) of others. See enclosure at end of letter." The enclosure was "the greater part of Maury Noble's monologue in the chapter called Symposium."[40] For this one scene, then, we have Fitzgerald's confession that the ideas expressed by the characters are his own. Maury Noble launches his monologue (which consumes about seven pages in the novel) by stating simply, "I think I shall tell you the story of my education." (252) The story turns out to be a rambling account of his ultra-sophisticated disillusion. Since there is no apparent function of the monologue other than to give Maury Noble something "important to say," the ideas must rest on their own merit. Two paragraphs, which did not appear in the magazine version and which are, therefore, probably part of the interpolation sent to Edmund Wilson, give the general tenor of the whole:

"For it seemed to me that there was no ultimate goal for man. Man was beginning a grotesque and bewildered fight with nature— nature, that by the divine and magnificent accident had brought us to where we could fly in her face. She had invented ways to

[40] Fitzgerald, "Letters to Friends," *The Crack-Up*, p. 256.

rid the race of the inferior and thus give the remainder strength to
fill her higher – or, let us say, her more amusing – though still
unconscious and accidental intentions. And, actuated by the
highest gifts of the enlightenment, we were seeking to circumvent
her. In this republic I saw the black beginning to mingle with the
white – in Europe there was taking place an economic catastrophe
to save three or four diseased and wretchedly governed races from
the one mastery that might organize them for material prosperity.

"We produce a Christ who can raise up the leper – and presently
the breed of the leper is the salt of the earth. If any one can find
any lesson in that, let him stand forth." (255)

There is an ugly note of racism sounded here that is of a piece with
Gloria's outburst against the mob. It is astonishing to find that Fitzgerald considered these ideas significant, and, indeed, claimed them as
his own. It would appear that he wanted his reader's sympathies to lie
where, too often, they could not: with the superficial but sometimes
sinister philosophy of his characters.

When Fitzgerald said in his letter to Edmund Wilson that he had
interpolated some recent ideas of his own "and (possibly) of others"
in the Maury Noble monologue, it is probable that chief among "the
others" was H. L. Mencken. In his review of Mencken's *Prejudices:
Second Series*, Fitzgerald chose one portion of the first essay, "The National Letters," for particular praise: "the section of the essay devoted to
the Cultural Background rises to brilliant analysis. Here again he is
thinking slowly, he is on comparatively fresh ground, he brings the
force of his clarity and invention to bear on the subject – passes beyond
his function as a critic of the arts and becomes a reversed Cato of a civilization."[41] This section of "The National Letters" expresses an attitude
that seems to underlie most of the ultra-sophisticated philosophizing
in *The Beautiful and Damned*, and particularly in Maury Noble's monologue. Mencken said, in part: "Democracy, obliterating the old aristocracy, has left only a vacuum in its place; in a century and a half it
has failed either to lift up the mob to intellectual autonomy and dignity
or to purge the plutocracy of its inherent stupidity and swinishness."
He bemoaned the lack in the United States "of a civilized aristocracy,
secure in its position, animated by an intelligent curiosity, skeptical of
all facile generalizations, superior to the sentimentality of the mob, and
delighting in the battle of ideas for its own sake."[42] At one point in *The
Beautiful and Damned*, Fitzgerald seems to indicate that his novel is an
attempt to create the kind of aristocracy for which Mencken called:

[41] Fitzgerald, "The Baltimore Anti-Christ," *op. cit.*, p. 80.
[42] Mencken, *Prejudices: Second Series*, pp. 65–78.

"A simple healthy leisure class it was – the best of the men not unpleasantly undergraduate... the women, of more than average beauty, fragilely athletic, somewhat idiotic as hostesses but charming and infinitely decorative as guests. Sedately and gracefully they danced the steps of their selection in the balmy tea hours, accomplishing with a certain dignity the movements so horribly burlesqued by clerk and chorus girl the country over." (191–92) Mencken would have missed in this "healthy leisure class" of *The Beautiful and Damned* an interest – not to say a delight – in ideas; perhaps Fitzgerald thought that he made up amply for that lack with such interpolations as the Maury Noble monologue. Whether or not Fitzgerald was consciously attempting to create an aristocracy patterned after that delineated by Mencken is not so important, however, as the painfully obvious fact that he conceived the "aristocratic" society of which Anthony and Gloria formed a part as far more significant than it was or than the reader could possibly imagine it to be.

As a result, probably, of Fitzgerald's inability to evaluate his material objectively or to make it conform to a "general scheme," the ending of *The Beautiful and Damned* points up the novel's primary defects. Apparently Fitzgerald had difficulty drawing his narrative to a conclusion. Edmund Wilson saw the first draft of *The Beautiful and Damned* and said later that it "culminated in a carnival of disaster for which the reader was imperfectly prepared; Fitzgerald ruined his characters wholesale with a set of catastrophes so arbitrary that beside them, the worst perversities of Hardy were like the working of natural laws."[43] Besides involving a number of improbalities, this ending would have muddled Fitzgerald's theme to an even greater extent than it is.

The conclusion of *The Beautiful and Damned* which Fitzgerald finally hit upon is ambiguous. In the final scene aboard ship, some fellow passengers report that Anthony has "been a little crazy, they say, ever since he got his money," and that Gloria looks "sort of dyed and unclean." (448) Anthony's mind, the only resource he has for defense of his perverse philosophy, has been dulled; and Gloria's beauty, the only source of her charm, is fading. But they have won the trial contesting old Adam Patch's will and, with it, a large fortune. Anthony seems to be glorying in some kind of triumph in the closing scene:

> Only a few months before people had been urging him to give
> in, to submit to mediocrity, to go to work. But he had known that
> he was justified in his way of life – and he had stuck it out stanchly.
> Why, the very friends who had been most unkind had come to

43 Wilson, "The Literary Spotlight: F. Scott Fitzgerald," *op. cit.*, p. 24.

respect him, to know he had been right all along. Had not the Lacys and the Merediths and the Cartwright-Smiths called on Gloria and him at the Ritz-Carlton just a week before they sailed?

Great tears stood in his eyes, and his voice was tremulous as he whispered to himself.

"I showed them," he was saying. "It was a hard fight, but I didn't give up and I came through!" (449)

The difficulty in interpreting the intention of this scene is suggested by the variety of meanings ascribed to it by reviewers and critics. One reviewer commented, "the parable ends with a glorious ironical punch. Gloria is punished by the mere loss of youth and beauty; Anthony by the utter fatuity of wealth."[44] Contrast this judgment with Carl Van Doren's in his review: "Nor does it increase the reality of the fall to allow him [Anthony] a penultimate hour of madness and an ultimate hour of victory, his millions in his hand."[45] Another critic has written: "By every law *The Beautiful and Damned* should have been a tragedy, the victims damned indeed; yet at the conclusion Fitzgerald welched, and permitted his pitiful pair to have the alleviations of some thirty millions of dollars, and his hero tell the readers he had won out."[46] Has Anthony actually been triumphant, and, if so, against what? He has won his law suit and a fortune, but how is this victory any justification for his philosophy? The money allows him to continue to do nothing, but does it prove, as he asserts, his contention that life is meaningless? Or perhaps the significance of this final scene lies beneath the surface. Perhaps the reader is supposed to see irony in Anthony's pitifully defiant claim of triumph. In any case, Fitzgerald's theme does not emerge clearly. The theme of the meaninglessness of life tends to neutralize the theme of revolt. By representing the moral disintegration of those who believe that life is meaningless, Fitzgerald does not support their philosophy, nor by showing the deterioration of those who revolt does he give significance to their rebellion. Fitzgerald's apparently mixed purposes and ambiguous sympathies in the novel render impossible a clear development of the theme.

In *The Beautiful and Damned*, Fitzgerald uses the conventional omniscient point of view, telling the story primarily through the eyes of Anthony and Gloria but not hesitating, when occasion requires, to

[44] H. W. Boynton, "Flashlight and Flame," *The Independent and the Weekly Review*, CVIII (April 22, 1922), 397.

[45] Carl Van Doren, "The Roving Critic," *The Nation*, CXIV (March 15, 1922), 318.

[46] Paul Rosenfeld, "F. Scott Fitzgerald," *op. cit.*, p. 321.

reveal the thoughts or adopt the perspective of various minor characters. Fitzgerald himself is a less obtrusive author than in *This Side of Paradise*, but he still occasionally addresses himself directly to the reader. In the stage directions of one of his scenes (written, as in *This Side of Paradise*, like the scene of a play), "A Flash-Back in Paradise," he informs the reader of "a conversation that took many hours and of which I can give only a fragment here." (28) Although this instance is the only case of Fitzgerald's entering the story in the first person singular (except for the ending which appeared in the magazine version), he maintains an easy informality with the reader throughout which lets him know that the author is never far behind the scenes. For example, in the initial description of Anthony, Fitzgerald says in an aside to the reader: "As you first see him he wonders frequently whether he is not without honor and slightly mad... the occasions being varied, of course, with those in which he thinks himself... somewhat more significant than any one else he knows." (3)

In tracing the moral disintegration of Gloria and Anthony, Fitzgerald portrays their internal dramas alternately: he allows himself the privilege of seeing into either of their minds whenever it suits narrative purposes. Up until Anthony's marriage to Gloria, the story is related largely through his consciousness. In representing the wedding itself, Fitzgerald portrays the meditations of both Anthony and Gloria in a simple but novel way. One block of his narrative he entitles "Anthony"; the protagonist is first conscious of "five hundred eyes boring through the back of his cutaway" until he notices "the clergyman's inappropriately bourgeois teeth." (155) Anthony attempts to force himself to feel the conventional emotions of a man being married but discovers such emotions impossible to experience. The teeth of the clergyman perversely capture his attention and he wonders whether the clergyman is married and "if a clergyman could perform his own marriage service." (155) As his thoughts finally wander to the girl at his side, Anthony's section of narrative ends abruptly with the terse observation, "He was married." (155) Immediately following is a section entitled "Gloria," which represents her mental and emotional response to the wedding ceremony: "So many, such mingled emotions, that no one of them was separable from the others... She was beyond all conscious perceptions. Only a sense, colored with delirious wild excitement, that the ultimately important was happening." (155) By such a simple device, Fitzgerald has succeeded, without cluttering his narrative with awkward transitions, in representing the consciousness of both his main characters during a moment of crucial importance in their lives.

But Fitzgerald does not resort to this device again. When he wishes to dramatize the reactions of his two leading characters to a single event, he represents alternately the thoughts of one and, after an appropriate transitional phrase, the meditations of the other. The scene in which old Adam Patch accidentally discovers his nephew and niece throwing a wild drunken party covers an event which would obviously frighten and dismay both Anthony and Gloria: they have, by horrifying the old man with their debauchery, endangered their inheritance of his immense fortune to which they have looked forward with eagerness. This scene is done in the form of a play, with dialogue and stage directions, and the "internal" reactions of Gloria and Anthony, except as indicated by speeches, are not represented. Immediately after this scene, under the sub-title "Retrospect," Fitzgerald begins his dramatization of the intense emotional response of both Gloria and Anthony to this pivotal event in their lives with a striking figure: "In this extremity they were like two goldfish in a bowl from which all the water had been drawn; they could not even swim across to each other." (276) In some three paragraphs devoted to her reaction, Gloria reviews in brief her entire married life, concluding: "It was only recently that she perceived that in spite of her adoration of him [Anthony], her jealousy, her servitude, her pride, she fundamentally despised him – and her contempt blended indistinguishably with her other emotions." (277) Following a simple transition ("On Anthony's part...") Fitzgerald devotes a parallel three paragraphs to the despair of Anthony's reaction: "There were times when he felt that if he were not left absolutely alone he would go mad – there were a few times when he definitely hated her." (277) There is a grim but artistic symmetry in the way in which both Anthony and Gloria turn their hatred upon each other. The closing paragraph of this section, like the opening, represents them together, driven by their terror into a tenuous reconciliation: "Then, on the August morning after Adam Patch's unexpected call, they awoke, nauseated and tired, dispirited with life, capable only of one pervasive emotion – fear." (278) It is with neatness and balance that Fitzgerald portrays the complex hysteria with which Anthony and Gloria react to the impending loss of a fortune nearly theirs.

At the end of *The Beautiful and Damned* Fitzgerald resorts to an unusual and effective device in his point of view. In the final scene when Gloria and Anthony are aboard ship, Fitzgerald shifts to the perspective of two fellow passengers:

> ... the young man in the plaid cap crossed the deck quickly and spoke to the pretty girl in yellow.

"That's him," he said, pointing to a bundled figure seated in a wheel-chair near the rail. "That's Anthony Patch. First time he's been on deck."

"Oh – that's him?"

"Yes. He's been a little crazy, they say, ever since he got his money, four or five months ago. You see, the other fellow, Shuttle-worth, the religious fellow, the one that didn't get the money, he locked himself up in a room in a hotel and shot himself –"

"Oh, he *did* –"

"But I guess Anthony Patch don't care much. He got his thirty million. And he's got his private physician along in case he doesn't feel just right about it. Has *she* been on deck?" he asked.

The pretty girl in yellow looked around cautiously.

"She was here a minute ago. She had on a Russian sable coat that must have cost a small fortune." She frowned and then added decisively: "I can't stand her, you know. She seems sort of – sort of dyed and *unclean*, if you know what I mean. Some people just have that look about them whether they are or not." (447–48)

In this very brief scene, Fitzgerald informs the reader of the important events that have taken place in the four or five months since Anthony and Gloria won the trial, yet he does it *scenically* or *dramatically*. But the real value of the scene lies in its portrayal of Anthony and Gloria not as they envision themselves nor as the author views them, but as two detached, disinterested persons see them. The reader feels that this glimpse of Anthony and Gloria is authentic – that he would see them in precisely this way were he there. The disabled Anthony is "a little crazy" and the ostentatiously dressed Gloria looks "sort of dyed and unclean"; their deterioration is made the more complete because it becomes the subject of common gossip.

There is much less variety in the handling of the point of view in *The Beautiful and Damned* than there was in *This Side of Paradise*. The poetry is missing, or, perhaps, has become a more integral part of the style; and there are no stream-of-consciousness passages in *The Beautiful and Damned*. There seems, however, to be less of the author in the second novel: he does not intrude in so crude a fashion as he formerly did. And the devices resorted to in manipulating and shifting the point of view seem to be much more in response to the demands of subject and theme than those used in *This Side of Paradise*. Fitzgerald seems to be yielding to the needs of the story rather than attempting to impress the reader with his virtuosity, as formerly. *The Beautiful and Damned* reveals, then, an advance in technique, inasmuch as it represents the subjection of method to action, motivating purpose, or theme.

In the representation of events, as in the handling of point of view, Fitzgerald was confronted with a more complex problem in *The Beautiful and Damned* than in *This Side of Paradise*. In addition to dealing with not one but two major characters, he was dramatizing a more unified line of action. Whereas in *This Side of Paradise*, as the reviewer for the *Publisher's Weekly* said, there was no "story in the regular sense" in that there was no single "plot" with a beginning, middle, and end, in *The Beautiful and Damned* there is a central line of action: the moral and physical disintegration of Anthony and Gloria through their ruthless search for pleasure and, more particularly, through the failure of the fulfillment of their "great expectations."

There is no attempt in *The Beautiful and Damned* to rearrange the normal chronological order of events or to withhold account of any incident to create suspense. In some sixteen pages of conventional exposition opening the novel, Fitzgerald begins with a general description of Anthony's character, and then, under the subtitle "A Worthy Man and His Gifted Son," (4) describes Anthony's ancestry. Anthony's own life up to the opening of the story is briefly summarized under "Past and Person of the Hero," (6) followed by a description of Anthony's present living quarters under "The Reproachless Apartment," (10) and a "preliminary" statement of his philosophy under "Nor Does He Spin." (12) Finally, Fitzgerald launches the action of the story with a specific event in a particular setting under the subtitle, "Afternoon." (16) From this point on the events are related in the order of their happening with the one major exception of Gloria's experiences while Anthony is away in the army. Following the chapter devoted to Anthony's army experiences, Fitzgerald begins: "On the night when Anthony had left for Camp Hooker one year before..." (359) But Fitzgerald's divergence from the chronological order seems to be dictated more by necessity through the separation of his two major characters than by artistic considerations.

As in *This Side of Paradise*, Fitzgerald still makes frequent use of subtitles within his chapters, but not so much to present "snapshots" or episodes only loosely related to the story as to separate one event in the main line of action from another. In *The Beautiful and Damned* Fitzgerald still makes frequent use of the dramatic scene, but not always at the most appropriate times. For example, in the scene called "The Ushers," immediately preceding the wedding of Anthony and Gloria, the reader is informed that there are "six young men in Cross Patch's library growing more and more cheery under the influence of Mumm's Extra Dry, set surreptitiously in cold pails by the bookcases." (151)

There follows a series of speeches introduced by "The First Young Man," "The Second Young Man," and so on up to the "Sixth Young Man." Then, gradually, Fitzgerald substitutes names for numbers until four of the speakers are identified. Out of the four names, however, the reader recognizes only two – Dick Caramel and Maury Noble. Instead of achieving the effect of rapid and witty conversation which he was apparently trying for, Fitzgerald actually confuses the reader. And it would be difficult to justify the elaborate representation of an event of such minor significance to the plot or theme.

The charge of insignificance cannot, however, be laid against one of the "drama" scenes – that in which old Adam Patch suddenly drops in on the "fast" party thrown by Anthony and Gloria. Although this event is an important turning point in the action and seems to be one which would normally lend itself easily to dramatization, it is difficult to understand why Fitzgerald used the dramatic form. In the stage directions he takes liberties with the method which presumably he should not be allowed: he interrupts the conversation at one point and says, "During the ensuing testament, left to be filled in by the reader with such phrases as 'Saw with his own eyes,' 'Splendid spirit of France,' and 'Salvation of civilization,' Maury sits with lowered eyelids, dispassionately bored" (265); he reveals the minds of his characters, on one occasion informing the reader that "Dick fatuously imagines that Paramore is someone he has previously met in Anthony's house" (267); he even comments, for the benefit of the reader, on the importance of things to come when, before the entrance of Adam Patch, he exclaims "But the grotesque, the unbelievable, the histrionic incident is about to occur, one of those incidents in which life seems set upon the passionate imitation of the lowest forms of literature." (274) Fitzgerald utilizes the so-called stage directions for revelations and comment of the kind normally confined to conventional narration, and consequently dissipates whatever effect he might have achieved by presenting the scene as pure drama. There is an unrelieved "cuteness" in this scene as well as in others throughout *The Beautiful and Damned* that does not quite succeed as either humor or wit.

One of the "drama" scenes, "A Flash-Back in Paradise," apparently represents Fitzgerald's effort to prepare the reader for Gloria's overpowering beauty. The setting is the "outdoor waiting-room of winds and stars" where Beauty "has been sitting for a hundred years, at peace in the contemplation of herself." (27) Beauty, says Fitzgerald, "was incomprehensible, for, in her, soul and spirit were one – the beauty of her body was the essence of her soul. She was that unity sought for by philosophers through many centuries." (27) Beauty begins a conversation with "a voice that was in the white wind," and learns that she is "to be born again." (27) The Voice tells her that she is to go to "the most opulent, most gorgeous land on earth – a land whose wisest are but little wiser than its dullest." (28) Beauty wants to know what she is going to be:

> The voice: At first it was thought that you would go this time as an actress in the motion-pictures but, after all, it's not advisable. You will be disguised during your fifteen years as what is called a "Susciety gurl."
> Beauty: What's that?
> (*There is a new sound in the wind which must for our purposes be interpreted as The Voice scratching its head.*)
> The Voice: (*at length*) It's a sort of bogus aristocrat. (29)

The Voice proceeds to tell Beauty that she will be known as "a ragtime kid, a flapper, a jazz-baby, and a baby vamp." (29) The reader learns finally that Beauty has descended, in this extraordinary fashion, on Gloria. Fitzgerald was probably doubtful (and rightfully so) about this episode. In his letter to John Peale Bishop regarding Bishop's review of *The Beautiful and Damned*, Fitzgerald remarked, "If you think my 'Flashback in Paradise' in Chap. I [*sic*] is like the elevated moments of D. W. Griffith say so."[47] If Fitzgerald meant this scene to be humorous (and evidently the "Voice scratching its head" was meant to evoke laughter), perhaps he partially succeeded; but it is a sophomoric humor out of place in context. Although the episode might astonish the reader with the "cuteness" and eccentricity of the imagination of the author, the scene seems to conflict with the novel's generally serious purpose and realistic tone.

In the "panoramic" portions of the narrative, Fitzgerald has not made as much use of "snapshots" or of letters as in his first novel, and there are no book-lists to indicate the intellectual development of Anthony or Gloria. There is one new "panoramic" device which Fitzgerald uses effectively – Gloria's diary.[48] After presenting Anthony's back-

---

[47] Fitzgerald, "Letters to Friends," *The Crack-Up*, p. 258.

[48] Oscar Cargill, in *Intellectual America* (p. 349), said that "the advancement of the story by the inclusion of passages from Gloria's diary in *The Beautiful and Damned*... [was] suggested by the work of Joyce." Joyce used the diary- device at the end of *A Portrait of the Artist as a Young Man*, and Fitzgerald was probably familiar with the novel. But Fitzgerald had another possible source for the diary. Mrs. F. Scott Fitzgerald, in her review of *The Beautiful and Damned* ("Friend Husband's Latest," New York Tribune, April 2, 1922, p. 11) said, "It seems to me that on one page I recognized a portion of an old diary of mine which mysteriously disappeared shortly after my marriage, and also scraps of letters which, though considerably edited, sound to me vaguely familiar."

ground and past at the opening of the novel in conventional exposition, devoting many pages to it before Anthony meets Gloria, Fitzgerald reviews Gloria's past by portraying her as reading her diary:

> Yet as she thumbed over the pages the eyes of many men seemed to look out at her from their half-obliterated names. With one she had gone to New Haven for the first time – in 1908, when she was sixteen and padded shoulders were fashionable at Yale – she had been flattered because "Touch down" Michaud had "rushed" her all evening. She sighed, remembering the grown-up satin dress she had been so proud of and the orchestra playing "Yama-yama, My Yama Man" and "Jungle-Town." So long ago! – the names: Eltynge Reardon, Jim Parsons, "Curly" McGregor, Kenneth Cowan, "Fish-eye" Fry (whom she had liked for being so ugly), Carter Kirby – he had sent her a present; so had Tudor Baird; – Marty Reffer, the first man she had been in love with for more than a day, and Stuart Holcome, who had run away with her in his automobile and tried to make her marry him by force. And Larry Fenwick, whom she had always admired because he had told her one night that if she wouldn't kiss him she could get out of his car and walk home. What a list! (144–45)

The diary is a natural selective device in itself and Gloria's nostalgic recollections, involving the crises and excitements of her past love-life, represent an even more rigorous selection. By this device, Fitzgerald has succeeded in a very short space in evoking a comprehensive and vivid impression of Gloria's extensive and "intense" past.

Although *The Beautiful and Damned* contains some remnants of the documentary novel, it is, technically, an advance over *This Side of Paradise*. When one reviewer charged that Fitzgerald's "irrelevance destroys his design,"[49] he praised as well as condemned by implying that the book had a design to be destroyed. *This Side of Paradise*, episodic, with no central line of action, has as its only unifying element the central character, Amory Blaine, and almost anything that happens to him is of importance in his story. *The Beautiful and Damned*, on the other hand, contains a central and unifying action which may serve as a basis for judgment of relevancy. Although *The Beautiful and Damned* is no novel of *selection*, it is an advance toward selection. Technical devices are used in it with much more sense of purpose than those in *This Side of Paradise*. Fitzgerald seems to have developed an awareness of the crucial relationship of technique to theme and plot, and most of the technical devices to which he resorts seem properly adapted to subject or theme. *The Beautiful and Damned* is, for Fitzgerald, a novel of transition.

[49] Vivian Shaw, "This Side of Innocence," *The Dial*, LXXII (April, 1922), 421.

3: *THE GREAT GATSBY*

A NOVEL OF SELECTION

I. THE ART OF MAGIC SUGGESTIVENESS

Upon learning that he was to be featured in "The Literary Spotlight" of *The Bookman* in March, 1922, Fitzgerald wrote to Edmund Wilson, "I deduce that this is your doing. My curiosity is at fever-heat – for God's sake send me a copy immediately."[1] In this early critical estimate of Fitzgerald, Wilson stressed the lack of form, the lack of basic purpose in the first two novels: Fitzgerald, he said, "has been given imagination without intellectual control of it; he has been given a desire for beauty without an aesthetic ideal; and he has been given a gift for expression without any ideas to express."[2] It is difficult to overestimate the seriousness with which Fitzgerald probably regarded Wilson's criticism. Having met as undergraduates at Princeton, he and Wilson were close friends throughout Fitzgerald's lifetime; in "The Crack-Up," 1936, Fitzgerald confessed, "For twenty years a certain man had been my intellectual conscience. That was Edmund Wilson."[3] Wilson's 1922 essay in *The Bookman* must have caused Fitzgerald to reconsider soberly and deeply his entire approach to the novel as an art form. Sometime between *The Beautiful and Damned* (1922) and *The Great Gatsby* (1925), Fitzgerald won "intellectual control" over his imagination, and, in doing so, abandoned one literary tradition and embraced another.

The development of Fitzgerald's "aesthetic ideal" can be traced to a certain extent in the scattered book reviews which he wrote during this period. In two early reviews which appeared in May, 1922, there is little evidence that Fitzgerald had any clear criteria with which to judge the novels he was discussing. He said of John V. A. Weaver's *Margey Wins the Game*, "The cross-section of gay Chicago is well done. The people, hastily sketched, are types, but convincing as such."[4] Shane Leslie's *The Oppidan* elicited the comment, "The book interested me enormously. Mr. Leslie has a sharp eye for the manners of his age."[5] Such general statements as these, concerned, to a great degree, with the exactness with which the works reproduced or copied life, reveal

---

[1] Fitzgerald, "Letters to Friends," *The Crack-Up*, p. 257.
[2] Wilson, "The Literary Spotlight: F. Scott Fitzgerald," *op. cit.*, p. 20.
[3] Fitzgerald, "The Crack-Up," *The Crack-Up*, p. 79.
[4] F. Scott Fitzgerald, "Margey Wins the Game," *New York Tribune*, May 7, 1922, p. 7.
[5] F. Scott Fitzgerald, "Homage to the Victorians," *New York Tribune*, May 14, 1922, p. 6.

that Firzgerald was not yet conscious of technique as a basic or central problem in the novel.

Fitzgerald found Woodward Boyd's *The Love Legend*, which he reviewed in October, 1922, "a good book" and advised the reader to "put it upon the shelf with 'Babbitt' and 'The Bright Shawl' and watch and pray for more such entertainment." The reason for such high praise was the novel's photographic copying of life, – as it was "easily the best picture of Chicago since 'Sister Carrie.'" But Fitzgerald pointed out some interesting "masculine defects" in the novel: "Intellectual curiosity in what amounts to a riot, solid blocks of strong words fitted into consecutive pages like bricks, a lack of selective delicacy, and, sometimes, a deliberately blunted perception." This comment is the first that revealed Fitzgerald's awareness of "selective delicacy" as a necessary principle in fiction; the phrase suggests the gradual change his concept of the novel was undergoing. Also indicative of his developing awareness was his attempt to defend the lack of form in *The Love Legend*: "In first novels this [formlessness] is permissible, perhaps even to be encouraged, as the lack of a pattern gives the young novelist more of a chance to assert his or her individuality, which is the principal thing."[6] Basing a critical judgment on the concept that the assertion of the author's "individuality" is the "principal thing" seems to be similar to (and as arbitrary as) Wells's defense of irrelevance "if the writer's mood is happy." But, in the very fact that he assumed the burden of justifying the absence of form, by pronouncing formlessness "permissible" in a beginning novelist, Fitzgerald demonstrated his growing concern for the *artistic* nature of the novel.

It was not, however, until he reviewed Grace Flandrau's *Being Respectable* in March, 1923, that Fitzgerald revealed a comprehensive understanding of the two "methods," *saturation* and *selection*, and suggested his growing preference for and belief in the superiority of *selection*. He called *Being Respectable* "something native and universal, clumsy in its handling of an enormous quantity of material; something which can be called a document, but can in no sense be dismissed as such." Although he thought the writing "solid throughout, and sometimes beautiful," he objected to the lack of anything "to draw together the entire novel," and he noted the lack of *selection*: "Like Sinclair Lewis and Woodward Boyd, the author has little sense of selection – seems to have poured the whole story out in a flood." He objected also to the confusion in the manipulation of the point of view: "The book

---

[6] F. Scott Fitzgerald, "A Rugged Novel," *The Literary Review of the New York Evening Post*, October 28, 1922, pp. 143–44.

lacks the careful balance of 'Three Soldiers,' and it is not nearly so successful in handling three or four protagonists. It skips from character to character in a way that is often annoying." Having emphasized technique throughout his review of *Being Respectable*, Fitzgerald concluded: "But there it is, the newest and in some ways the best of those amazing documents which are (as Mencken might say) by H. G. Wells out of Theodore Dreiser, and which yet are utterly national and of today. And, when our Conrad or Joyce or Anatole France comes, such books as this will have cleared his way. Out of these enormous and often muddy lakes of sincere and sophisticated observation will flow the clear stream – if there is to be a clear stream at all."[7] The image of the clear stream flowing out of the muddy lake, embodying, apparently, Fitzgerald's newly conceived idea of the historical development of the novel in America, is an excellent figure: "muddy lakes" suggests the abundance of documentation in the saturation novel, and "clear stream" implies the lucid, central purpose of the novel of selection. The keenness of Fitzgerald's "sudden insight" is all the more appreciated when it is realized that he presented as examples two writers whom James had used for almost identical purposes in "The New Novel": H. G. Wells for *saturation* and Joseph Conrad for *selection*. It seems that Fitzgerald suddenly grasped for the first time the function of the novel as a work of art and the direction inevitable for the modern novel if it was to become (as Willa Cather hoped it would) "more varied and perfect than all the many novels that have gone before."

Prefacing his review of Thomas Boyd's *Through the Wheat*, May, 1923, with a quotation from Joseph Conrad's "Youth," Fitzgerald asserted, "So, in part, runs one of the most remarkable passages of English prose written these thirty years." He concluded his review by referring to still another work – Stephen Crane's masterpiece: "To my mind, this is not only the best combatant story of the great war, but also the best war book since 'The Red Badge of Courage.'" These titles, suggesting in themselves the new standards or criteria to which Fitzgerald was turning, indicate his particular approach in appraising *Through the Wheat*: "At first the very exactitude of the detail makes one expect no more than another piece of expert reporting, but gradually the thing begins to take on significance and assume a definite and arresting artistic contour." In his attempt to define the "artistic contour" of the novel, Fitzgerald significantly discovered that it exhibited "delicacy" of selection designed to render every detail consistently relevant: "There is a

[7] Fitzgerald, "Minnesota's Capital in the Role of Main Street," *The Literary Digest International Book Review*, I (March, 1923), 35–36.

fine unity about it all... The effect is cumulative in the sheerest sense; there are no skies and stars and dawn pointed out to give significance to the insignificant or to imply a connection where there is no connection. There are no treasured-up reactions to aesthetic phenomena poured along the pages, either for sweetening purposes or to endow the innately terrible with a higher relief. The whole book is written in the light of one sharp emotion and hence it is as a work of art rather than as a text-book for patrioteer or pacifist that the book is arresting."[8] In pointing out the "fine unity" achieved through the rigorous suppression of the insignificant in *Through the Wheat*, Fitzgerald was demonstrating the crucial importance in fiction of technique. His closing remark, classifying the book "as a work of art rather than as a textbook," conclusively reveals that Fitzgerald had developed an allegiance to a tradition in fiction directly opposed to that in which he discovered himself at the beginning of his career.

In the process of abandoning the "slice-of-life" type of novel and developing an aesthetic ideal with "selective delicacy" as a major principle, Fitzgerald had to repudiate his old literary models and attach himself to new. A letter to John Peale Bishop discloses that by the winter of 1924–25 Fitzgerald's early enthusiasm for Mackenzie and Wells was a thing of the perhaps nostalgic but nevertheless irrecoverable past: "We're just back from Capri where I sat up (tell Bunny) half the night talking to my old idol Compton Mackenzie. Perhaps you met him. I found him cordial, attractive and pleasantly mundane. You get no sense from him that he feels his work has gone to pieces. He's not pompous about his present output. I think he's just tired. The war wrecked him as it did Wells and many of that generation."[9] The change attributed to Wells and Mackenzie was in reality a basic shift in Fitzgerald's own perspective on the novel. Although early in his career he had borrowed extensively in both ideas and method from them, the old idols were no longer able to contribute anything to his craft. Fitzgerald was also viewing H. L. Mencken, who had shaped so many of his attitudes in *The Beautiful and Damned*, with a more critical eye. In an essay on contemporary writers (1926), Fitzgerald asserted: "What Mencken felt the absence of, what he wanted, and justly, back in 1920, got away from him, got twisted in his hand. Not because the 'literary revolution' went beyond him but because his idea had always been ethical rather

[8] Fitzgerald, "Under Fire," *The Literary Review of the New York Evening Post*, May 26, 1923, p. 715.
[9] Fitzgerald, "Letters to Friends," *The Crack-Up*, p. 268.

than aesthetic."[10] Although this essay appeared in May, 1926, it seems clear that Fitzgerald believed, by the time he wrote *The Great Gatsby*, that Mencken's concept of the novel was fundamentally in error.

It would be gratifying to be able to demonstrate that Fitzgerald changed "sides" in the Wells-James controversy, shifting from the idea of technique in the novel as primarily *saturation* to the concept of *selection* under the influence and guidance of the master – Henry James. Indeed, many of the reviewers, commenting on the technique of *The Great Gatsby*, turned to Henry James as an appropriate point of comparison. The reviewer for the *New York Times Book Review* claimed, "In the method of telling, 'The Great Gatsby' is reminiscent of Henry James's 'Turn of the Screw.'"[11] Carl Van Vechten, in *The Nation*, asserted, "This character [Gatsby], and the theme of the book in general, would have appealed to Henry James.... Mr. Fitzgerald has chosen, as James so frequently chose, to see his story through the eyes of a spectator."[12] And we have already noted that in a letter to Fitzgerald, T. S. Eliot linked *Gatsby* with the name of Henry James.

There exists no evidence, however, to suggest, that Fitzgerald was directly influenced by Henry James. In his discussion of "The Lees of Happiness" in that eccentric table of contents of *Tales of the Jazz Age*, Fitzgerald had referred to "melodramas carefully disguised by early paragraphs in Jamesian manner which hint dark and subtle complexities to follow." He had then attempted, rather unsuccessfully, to parody the involved and convolute James style: "The case of Shaw McPhee, curiously enough, had no bearing on the almost incredible attitude of Martin Sulo. This is parenthetical and, to at least three observers, whose names for the present I must conceal, it seems probable, etc., etc., etc."[13] Fitzgerald still held the mild intolerance for James suggested by this parody when he wrote to his daughter in July, 1938: "I certainly wouldn't begin Henry James with *The Portrait of a Lady*, which is in his 'late second manner' and full of mannerisms. Why don't you read *Roderick Hudson* or *Daisy Miller* first?"[14] Fitzgerald himself had probably not read this much of Henry James by the time he wrote *The Great Gatsby*. Edmund Wilson, in "Imaginary Conversations II: Mr. Van Wyck Brooks and Mr. Scott Fitzgerald," which appeared in *The*

[10] Fitzgerald, "How to Waste Material," *op. cit.*, p. 263.
[11] Edwin Clark, "Scott Fitzgerald Looks into Middle Age," *The New York Times Book Review*, XXX (April 19, 1925), 9.
[12] Carl Van Vechten, "Fitzgerald on the March," *The Nation*, CXX (May 20, 1925), 576.
[13] Fitzgerald, *Tales of the Jazz Age*, p. x.
[14] Fitzgerald, "Letters to Frances Scott Fitzgerald," *The Crack-Up*, p. 288.

New Republic in April, 1924, portrayed Fitzgerald as confessing to Van
Wyck Brooks, "'I don't know anything about James myself. I've never
read a word of him.'"[15] Although Fitzgerald, at the time of writing *The
Great Gatsby*, was apparently not under the direct influence of James, he
could have felt an immense indirect attraction through any number of
writers who themselves had gone to school to the master.

By 1925 Fitzgerald had transferred his former enthusiasm for Wells,
Mackenzie, and Mencken to a number of other writers. James Joyce,
Willa Cather, and most important, Joseph Conrad – all figured promi-
nently in the evolution of Fitzgerald's concept of the novel as a work
of art. The most intangible of all these influences was that of James
Joyce. One critic, Oscar Cargill, has asserted that "Fitzgerald was the
first Primitivist to be influenced by James Joyce."[16] Although we cannot
agree that Fitzgerald borrowed from Joyce all of the devices Cargill
claims (the dramatic scene, the diary), we can certainly agree that
Fitzgerald consciously felt the influence of Joyce. We may assume that
Fitzgerald was more or less familiar with *A Portrait of the Artist as a
Young Man*, as the title appears in one of Amory's reading lists in *This
Side of Paradise* (p. 224). In June, 1922, Fitzgerald wrote to Edmund
Wilson that he was reading Joyce's second novel: "I have *Ullyses* [*sic*]
from the Brick Row Bookshop & am starting it. I wish it was layed [*sic*]
in America – there is something about middle-class Ireland that de-
presses me inordinately – I mean gives me a sort of hollow, cheerless
pain. Half of my ancestors came from just such an Irish strata or
perhaps, a lower one. The book makes me feel appallingly naked."
In August, 1922, after Fitzgerald had apparently finished *Ulysses*, he
wrote Wilson again: "Am undecided about *Ullysses* [*sic*] application to
me – which is as near as I ever come to forming an impersonal judgment."[17] However undecided Fitzgerald was about *Ulysses*, (and we
cannot take his persistent misspelling of the title as a reliable indication
of his care in reading – he was always a bad speller), he regarded Joyce,
according to one of his 1923 book reviews, as an ideal model for the
American writer who would aid the "clear stream" to flow from the
"muddy lake" of documentary novels. In an interview with Charles C.
Baldwin in 1924, while Fitzgerald would have been writing *The Great
Gatsby*, he listed Joyce as one of a long list of "enthusiasms."[18]

[15] Edmund Wilson, "Imaginary Conversations II: Mr. Van Wyck Brooks and
Mr. Scott Fitzgerald," *The New Republic*, XXXVIII (April 30, 1924), 252.
[16] Oscar Cargill, *Intellectual America*, p. 346. See footnotes 60 and 64 of Chapter
One, footnote 48 of Chapter Two.
[17] Fitzgerald, "Letters to Friends," *The Crack-Up*, pp. 260–262.
[18] Charles C. Baldwin, in *The Men Who Make Our Novels* ([New York: Dodd, Mead

Since Fitzgerald's interest in Joyce was probably kindled by Edmund Wilson, it seems likely that Fitzgerald would have shared or at least have known Wilson's view of *Ulysses* published in November, 1922, in an essay devoted to the current trends in modern literature: "In 'Ulysses,'... though we have a section of the typical stream of consciousness in all its brokenness and triviality, its aimlessness and confusion, we have it organized within itself and brought into relation with the rest of the world. It is, in fact, a sort of Divine Comedy of the 20th century. Mr. Joyce has no theological, philosophical, or political system, but he at least manipulates his hero's reactions in obedience to a precise technical plan – in such a way as to make them cover in a day the whole of average human experience."[19] Probably Joyce's greatest contribution to Fitzgerald via Wilson was a sense of the necessity in fiction of "obedience to a precise technical plan." To suggest that Fitzgerald did not borrow specific technical devices is not to minimize Joyce's influence; Fitzgerald received much if he derived only a general sense of the vital importance of technique to the novel.

Some time after finishing and before publishing *The Great Gatsby*, Fitzgerald told Charles C. Baldwin what he had tried to accomplish in his new novel and how he had attempted to make it different from any of his previous work:

> "My third novel... is just finished and quite different from the other two in that it is an attempt at form and refrains carefully from trying to 'hit anything off.' Five years ago the new American novels needed comment by the author because they were facing a public that had had very little but trash for a hundred years – that is to say, the exceptions were few and far between and most of them were commercial failures. But now that there is an intelligent body of opinion guided by such men as Mencken, Edmund Wilson and Van Wyck Brooks, comment should be unnecessary; and the writer, if he has any aspirations toward art, should try to convey the feel of his scenes, places and people directly – as

and Company, 1924], p. 172), quotes Fitzgerald as saying, "'I am a pessimist, a communist (with Nietschean overtones), have no hobbies except conversation– and I am trying to repress that. My enthusiasms at present include Stravinski, Otto Braun, Mencken, Conrad, Joyce, the early Gertrude Stein, Chaplin and all books about that period which lies between the V and XV centuries.'"

[19] Wilson, "The Rag-Bag of the Soul," *op. cit.*, p. 238. In this same article, Wilson referred to Fitzgerald (p. 238): "... a quotation from a more conventional author who has yet caught something of the spirit of the time puts it even more clearly and briefly. 'I know myself but that is all,' cries one of Scott Fitzgerald's heroes, who has 'grown up to find all gods dead, all wars fought, all faiths in men shaken.' And that is precisely the point of view of the modern novelist or poet: 'I know myself but that is all.'"

Conrad does, as a few Americans (notably Willa Cather) are already trying to do."[20]

In this extended remark by Fitzgerald may be discovered four self-imposed "rules": that he should not try to "hit anything off"; that he, as author, should not comment in his novels; that he should make "an attempt at form"; and that he should "try to convey the feel of his scenes, places and people directly." Apparently to "hit things off" meant to indulge in smart, sophisticated philosophizing just for the sake of being clever, as Fitzgerald had done previously, especially in such scenes as the "Midnight Symposium" in *The Beautiful and Damned* (as one reviewer of that novel exclaimed: "If only Mr. Fitzgerald... could *feel* the difference between telling a story and hitting things off! If... he would only leave the latter art, or sport, to... the Menckens and the Nathans and the host of clever juniors who have no stories in them."[21]) Taking advantage of the looseness of the documentary novel (and of the right defended so vigorously by Wells), Fitzgerald in the role of vocal author had intruded frequently in his first two books. His repudiation of these two practices, together with his growing concern for form and his desire to evoke the feel of scenes "directly," shows that he had developed a keen concern for his craft as art.

Fitzgerald's assertion that it was the development, after 1920, of "an intelligent body of opinion" which made unnecessary the "comment by the author" is interesting but probably misleading. It is possible that the public was better prepared in 1925 to recognize the artistic worth of a novel than in 1920, primarily because of the critical achievements of Mencken, Edmund Wilson and Van Wyck Brooks – but Fitzgerald misplaced the emphasis. It was he, more than the reading public, who had developed and changed in that five year period, and, in pointing to Willa Cather and Joseph Conrad as examples of authors who were trying to be artists as well as writers, he was probably revealing the two novelists from whom he had derived his most intense "aspirations toward art."

Fitzgerald probably shared Thomas A. Boyd's enthusiasm for Willa Cather when he and Boyd were closely associated in early 1922 in St. Paul. In the same issue (and on the same page) of the St. Paul *Daily News* (March 5, 1922) in which Boyd's first article on Fitzgerald was published, appeared, in Boyd's literary column, a letter from Cather, which read in part, "But if he [the writer] is an artist he will not be

[20] Baldwin, *op. cit.*, p. 167.
[21] Boynton, "Flashlight and Flame," *op. cit.*, p. 397.

literal, because no artist can be. If he has the proper equipment to be a writer of fiction at all, he will never have to puzzle as to how far he should be literal; he has a selective machine in his brain that decides all that for him." At about this time Fitzgerald included the title of *My Ántonia* in a casual reference in one of his book reviews.[22] And it is quite probable that he saw Willa Cather's essay, "The Novel Démeublé," in *The New Republic*, April 12, 1922, especially since he spoke with some assurance of what she was "already trying to do." That issue of *The New Republic* with the entire literary supplement devoted to "The Novel of Tomorrow and the Scope of Fiction," beginning with a review of Percy Lubbock's *The Craft of Fiction*, could have given an immense impetus to Fitzgerald's meditations on the form of the novel. It was Willa Cather's essay in the symposium which stated the case most clearly for the novel as a work of art: "In any discussion of the novel, one must make it clear whether one is talking about the novel as a form of amusement, or as a form of art.... If the novel is a form of imaginative art, it cannot be at the same time a vivid and brilliant form of journalism." These distinctions Fitzgerald himself was attempting to suggest when he defined what the writer must do should he have "any aspirations toward art." If he read Willa Cather's essay, Fitzgerald learned much of the crucial importance of *selection* to the novel: she struck out against a "tasteless amplitude" and advised the writer to throw "all of the furniture out of the window."[23]

But Fitzgerald could have been influenced by Cather's novels themselves. Maxwell Geismar, apparently unaware of Fitzgerald's highly laudatory references to Cather, has suggested a close relationship between *The Great Gatsby* and *My Ántonia:*

> The similarity of theme and tone between the closing sections of *My Ántonia* and *The Great Gatsby* has probably not been sufficiently noticed by historians of literary craft: a similarity which extends through phrases and rhythms of the writing to the almost identical "dying-fall" of Fitzgerald's last sentence in Gatsby: "So we beat on, boats against the current, borne back ceaselessly into the past." It seems likely, that is, that Fitzgerald drew upon Willa Cather's work for his own development of the theme, although, since both writers also use the structural device of the "sensitive observer," there is the common influence of Henry James or the school of James.[24]

[22] Willa Cather's letter appeared in Thomas Boyd's "The Literary Punchbowl," *St. Paul Daily News*, March 5, 1922. Fitzgerald's reference to Cather appeared in "Tarkington's 'Gentle Julia,'" *St. Paul Daily News*, May 7, 1922.

[23] Cather, "The Novel Démeublé," *op. cit.*, pp. 5–6.

[24] Maxwell Geismar, *The Last of the Provincials* (Boston: Houghton Mifflin Co., 1947), p. 166.

The last sentence in *My Ántonia*, "Whatever we had missed, we possessed together the precious, the incommunicable past,"[25] is, as Geismar says, remarkably close in rhythm and feeling to (though different in meaning from) the last line of *The Great Gatsby*. And, as Geismar also points out, the device of the sensitive observer is common to both novels. In *My Ántonia*, there is an introduction in which the author meets an old friend, Jim Burden, on a train ride through the West. They begin reminiscing about their childhood, and their talk keeps "returning to a central figure, a Bohemian girl," Ántonia. Jim Burden tells the narrator that he has been writing down what he remembers about Ántonia and the narrator expresses an interest in reading this account:

> Months afterward, Jim called at my apartment one stormy winter afternoon, carrying a legal portfolio. He brought it into the sitting-room with him, and said, as he stood warming his hands,
> "Here is the thing about Ántonia. Do you still want to read it? I finished it last night. I didn't take time to arrange it; I simply wrote down pretty much all that her name recalls to me. I suppose it hasn't any form. It hasn't any title, either." He went into the next room, sat down at my desk and wrote across the face of the portfolio the word, "Ántonia." He frowned at this a moment, then prefixed another word, making it "My Ántonia." That seemed to satisfy him.[26]

By use of this device, Willa Cather is able to tell the story of Ántonia through the consciousness of a sensitive, sympathetic narrator, thereby effacing herself as author almost completely: Jim Burden, placed within the story, takes over most of the functions of (in the fictional sense, becomes) the author.

In reading *My Ántonia*, Fitzgerald could have gained a keen awareness of the possibilities of first person narration and of the advantages of filtering a story through a sensitive observer. But if the device of the observer arbitrarily imposed a *selection*, it also made possible a kind of *saturation*. When Willa Cather made Jim Burden say, "I simply wrote down pretty much all that her name recalls to me. I suppose it hasn't any form," she was granting herself a privilege of which she took full advantage. Jim Burden's statement establishes the probability of a rambling and discursive chronicle: it is logical that memories of Ántonia should bring back memories of other people, other events. In this fashion, the way is prepared for much of the narrative not strictly

---

[25] Willa Cather, *My Ántonia* (Boston: Houghton Mifflin Company, 1918), p. 419.
[26] *Ibid.*, pp. x–xi.

the story of Ántonia, such as the accounts of Lena Lingard, and Tiny Soderball. Whether such material, only indirectly relevant to the central story, is justified or not, the lack of form in the novel constitutes a real defect, and it is not probable that Fitzgerald developed his concern for form ("My third novel... is an attempt at form") from his reading of My Ántonia.

It is more likely that Fitzgerald suggested a relationship in achievement in form between Joseph Conrad and Willa Cather on the basis of a later novel which appeared in 1923 – A Lost Lady, the primary technique of which is similar to that used by Fitzgerald in The Great Gatsby. The central character of A Lost Lady is Marian Forrester, a woman of fine feeling and "culture," somewhat isolated in the relatively crude Middle Western town in which she lives with her husband, Captain Forrester, one of the last of the pioneer generation. The story is concerned with the gradual revelation of the coarse side of Marian Forrester's nature; her love affair with her husband's bachelor friend, Frank Ellinger; and her inability, after her husband's death, "to immolate herself, like the widows of all these great men, and die with the pioneer period to which she belonged... she preferred life on any terms."[27] In this novel, severe in form, highly compact and selective, the furniture is, indeed, thrown out the window: the focus is kept on Marian Forrester from beginning to end. The device which enabled the author to tell Marian Forrester's story so comprehensively yet selectively is the sympathetic observer through whom the events are filtered. Neil Herbert, a boy of the town who is fascinated by the charming and beautiful Mrs. Forrester, provides a natural selection for the story through his intermittent but significant contacts with the Forrester household; and his consciousness, because it reflects the reaction of the Middle Western town to Mrs. Forrester yet is sympathetic to her, is ideal for the interpretation of the events of the story. The Lost Lady is Neil Herbert's story inasmuch as he changes from an admiring to a disillusioned observer. His passing from ignorance to knowledge about life parallels and supplements Marian Forrester's decline from a position of grandeur to a place of tawdry cheapness. Neil Herbert functions in the story in relation to Marian Forrester very much as Nick Carraway functions in relation to Jay Gatsby in Fitzgerald's novel. In both instances the protagonist is seen through the eyes of a sympathetic observer in whom there is a change paralleling the alteration in the central character.

Although Neil Herbert acts like Nick Carraway, as a sympathetic observer, he also carries within himself an illusion similar to Gatsby's.

[27] Willa Cather, A Lost Lady (New York: Alfred A. Knopf, 1923), p. 169.

When, as a boy, Neil Herbert broke his arm and was carried into the nearby Forrester home: "[he] was thinking that he would probably never be in so nice a place again. The windows went almost down to the baseboard, like doors, and the closed green shutters let in streaks of sunlight that quivered on the polished floor and the silver things on the dresser. The heavy curtains were looped back with thick cords, like ropes. The marble-topped washstand was as big as a sideboard. The massive walnut furniture was all inlaid with pale-coloured woods." This material splendor, together with Marian Forrester's impressive charm and beauty, enabled Neil Herbert's active imagination to create an immense illusion: "He was proud... that at the first moment he had recognized her as belonging to a different world from any he had ever known."[28] Gatsby's dream parallels Neil's imaginative conception very closely: Daisy, excitingly beautiful and charming, in a material setting of wealth and splendor, belongs, in Gatsby's eyes, to a distant and inaccessible world. But the relation of Gatsby to Neil Herbert cannot be stressed too much, for Neil Herbert, when he discovered one morning by accident that Mrs. Forrester had entertained her lover in her bedroom overnight while her husband was away, lost his cherished illusion: "In that instant between stooping to the windowsill and rising, he had lost one of the most beautiful things in his life. Before the dew dried, the morning had been wrecked for him; and all subsequent mornings, he told himself bitterly. This day saw the end of that admiration and loyalty that had been like a bloom on his existence. He could never recapture it. It was gone, like the morning freshness of the flowers."[29] Neil Herbert's loss of his adolescent dream, whose gap was filled by a bitter and permanent disillusionment, signified his transition from boyhood to manhood. But Gatsby carried his dream to his death. The illusions of these two characters, though similar, serve vastly different thematic purposes.

It seems likely that the degree to which Fitzgerald was indebted to Willa Cather is greater than has been heretofore realized. From either Willa Cather's essay, "The Novel Démeublé," or from her novels, possibly from both, Fitzgerald probably learned a great deal about technique, especially about the manipulation of point of view, and about form and unity. But the similiarities of *A Lost Lady* and *The Great Gatsby* can be exaggerated: as shapely and compact as Willa Cather's novel is, Fitzgerald's surpasses it in unity and symmetry. *A Lost Lady* is related chronologically, covering a span of many years by the simple

[28] *Ibid.*, pp. 28–42.
[29] *Ibid.*, p. 86.

omission of irrelevant lapses of time; *The Great Gatsby*, although its actual narrative also covers a number of years, is dramatically narrated within the limits of one climactic summer. If Fitzgerald learned the rudiments of form from Willa Cather, he excelled her in his finest work.

Probably the greatest influence on Fitzgerald during the gestation period of *The Great Gatsby* was Joseph Conrad. When Fitzgerald, in August, 1922, said to Edmund Wilson, "See here... I want some new way of using the great Conradian vitality,"[30] he seemed to imply a seriousness belying the humorous context. There is no doubt that genuine gravity motivated the remarks in the March, 1923, book review in which Fitzgerald in effect ranked Conrad above Wells. Shortly after the publication of *The Great Gatsby*, Fitzgerald wrote to Edmund Wilson, "Mencken said (in a most enthusiastic letter received today) that the only fault was that the central story [of *The Great Gatsby*] was trivial and a sort of anecdote (that is because he has forgotten his admiration for Conrad and adjusted himself to the sprawling novel)."[31] By implication this casual remark linked Fitzgerald's work with Conrad's, and the suggestion is clear that the connection (as the work of both contrasted markedly with the sprawling novel) was one of technique.

When Fitzgerald said, "the writer, if he has any aspiration toward art, should try to convey the feel of his scenes, places and people directly – as Conrad does,"[32] he was echoing the one important statement which Conrad had made on his craft. And Fitzgerald confessed, when he wrote a preface for a reprint of *The Great Gatsby* in 1934, that just before writing his novel he had re-read Conrad's artistic manifesto: "Now that this book [*The Great Gatsby*] is being reissued, the author would like to say that never before did one try to keep his artistic conscience as pure as during the ten months put into doing it. Reading it over one can see how it could have been improved – yet without feeling guilty of any discrepancy from the truth, as far as I saw it; truth or rather the equivalent of the truth, the attempt at honesty of imagination. I had just re-read Conrad's preface to *The Nigger* [*of the Narcissus*]."[33] Since Fitzgerald remembered nine years later the impact of it on him and his novel, Conrad's preface to *The Nigger of the Narcissus*, a concise statement of his aims and purposes in the craft of fiction, must have impressed the American novelist deeply.[34] When he spoke of the attempt "to

[30] Fitzgerald, "Letters to Friends," *The Crack-Up*, p. 262.
[31] *Ibid.*, p. 270.
[32] Baldwin, *op. cit.*, p. 167.
[33] Fitzgerald, "Introduction," *The Great Gatsby* ("The Modern Library"; New York: Random House, 1934), pp. ix–x.
[34] In 1933, in an interesting article on the problems of the writer, Fitzgerald

convey the feel" of scenes, Fitzgerald was remembering the heart of that preface: "my task, which I am trying to achieve is, by the power of the written word to make you hear, to make you feel – it is, before all, to make you *see*. That – and no more, and it is everything."[35] To remove, as much as possible, all obstruction separating the reader from the *actual* scene is an ambitious and difficult task for the writer to set himself, and the way to success is not simple.

Conrad resorted to an analogy with the other arts for explanation: "It [writing] must strenuously aspire to the plasticity of sculpture, to the colour of painting, and to the magic suggestiveness of music – which is the art of arts." This "magic suggestiveness" (a term recalling Willa Cather's desire to make a single selected incident imply a volume of meaning) must derive, thought Conrad, from each situation or event, major or minor: "To snatch in a moment of courage, from the remorseless rush of time, a passing phase of life, is only the beginning of the task. The task approached in tenderness and faith is to hold up unquestioningly, without choice and without fear, the rescued fragment before all eyes in the light of a sincere mood. It is to show its vibration, its colour, its form; and through its movement, its form, and its colour, reveal the substance of its truth – disclose its inspiring secret: the stress and passion within the core of each convincing moment."[36] To the writer of the *saturation* novel, re-creation of "a passing phase of life" would be the main task; to the novelist of selection, the isolation of the action "is only the beginning."[37] He must "reveal the substance" of truth inherent within the situation, so that an individual moment can symbolize perhaps a multitude. In a comprehensive sense, Fitzgerald was indebted to Conrad for a new approach to his craft, for his high "aspirations toward art," the difficult art of "magic suggestiveness." He was indebted to Conrad also for more specific elements: for the use of style or language to reflect theme; for the use of the modified first person narra-

---

quoted from Conrad's preface ("One Hundred False Starts," *The Saturday Evening Post*, CCV [March 4, 1933], 66): "These old mistakes [discarded beginnings of stories] are now only toys–and expensive ones at that – give them a toy's cupboard and then hurry back into the serious business of my profession. Joseph Conrad defined it more clearly, more vividly than any man of our time:

'My task is by the power of the written word to make you hear, to make you feel – it is, before all, to make you see.'"

[35] Joseph Conrad, *The Nigger of the Narcissus: A Tale of the Sea* (New York: Doubleday, Doran & Company, Inc., 1935), p. xiv.

[36] *Ibid.*, pp. xiii–xiv.

[37] Ford Madox Ford, who collaborated for a time with Conrad, said in *Joseph Conrad: A Personal Remembrance* ([Boston: Little, Brown, and Company, 1924], p. 195): "We [Ford and Conrad] agreed that the whole of Art consists in selection."

tion; and for the use of deliberate "confusion" by the re-ordering of the chronology of events.

When he selected H. G. Wells to exemplify the novelist of *saturation* and Joseph Conrad to represent the novelist of *selection*, Henry James uncannily "predicted" the beginning and the end of Fitzgerald's artistic development. By the time Fitzgerald was ready to write *The Great Gatsby*, he could refer, with some distaste, to the "sprawling novel," and he could advocate, with some enthusiasm, "selective delicacy" in fictional technique. Wells, Mackenzie, and Mencken had been replaced in his critical esteem by Joyce, Cather, and Conrad, all novelists acutely conscious of the primary significance of technique. Fitzgerald had adopted Conrad's difficult and austere artistic credo: "Art is long and life is short, and success is very far off. And thus, doubtful of strength to travel so far, we talk a little about the aim – the aim of art, which, like life itself, is inspiring, difficult – obscured by mists."[38] Under the impact of a fresh re–reading of Conrad's preface to *The Nigger of the Narcissus*, Fitzgerald set about to "reveal the substance" of truth of his "rescued fragment," a fragment of the excitingly catastrophic 1920's. But before passing to an examination of the artistic embodiment of that truth, it will be useful to glance briefly at Fitzgerald's other literary productions since *The Beautiful and Damned*.

II. THOSE SAD YOUNG MEN: A MOVING EXPERIENCE

After the publication of *The Beautiful and Damned*, Fitzgerald's time and energy were dissipated in large measure by the writing and revision of his one play, *The Vegetable or From President to Postman*. The letters to Edmund Wilson during the latter part of 1922 trace a sad history of the play traveling from producer to producer, with much intermittent revision and high hope.[39] The play, which failed when it was finally produced but was published in April, 1923, is a fantasy with attempts at political satire which does not quite come off. Perhaps the primary contribution of *The Vegetable* to Fitzgerald's art was its putting an end to his tendency to cast important scenes in his novels in play form; after *The Vegetable*, he never again resorted to the method.

Fitzgerald's comments on his own short stories of this period indicate the dissatisfaction he felt when he thought he had fallen below his own high standards. He wrote to Edmund Wilson in October, 1924, "I really worked hard as hell last winter – but it was all trash and it nearly

---

[38] Conrad, *The Nigger of the Narcissus*, p. xv.
[39] Fitzgerald, "Letters to Friends," *The Crack-Up*, pp. 260–62.

broke my heart as well as my iron constitution." Twice during the winter of 1924–25 he wrote self-critically to John Peale Bishop: "No news except I now get 2000 a story and they grow worse and worse and my ambition is to get where I need write no more but only novels." And again: "I've done about 10 pieces of horrible junk in the last year... that I can never republish or bear to look at – cheap and without the spontaneity of my first work."[40] Fitzgerald obviously considered his short stories as pot-boilers, sapping his time and energy from the writing and revision of *The Great Gatsby*, in which he never lost faith. In one of the letters to Bishop, he had added: "But the novel I'm sure of. It's marvellous."

All the Sad Young Men (1926), which collected some ten of the short stories written and published before *The Great Gatsby*, is uneven in quality. Several of the stories were obviously written for the polular magazine audience. "Rags Martin-Jones and the Pr-nce of W-les," for example, creaks with its worn-out formula: rich, handsome boy meets rich, beautiful girl; boy, about to lose girl because she is bored and wants excitement, pulls extravagant trick on her for which she easily falls and which gives her desired excitement; boy, because of his ingenuity, wins girl. The material circumstances for such a formula can be varied infinitely:[41] in this story, John M. Chestnut, whose beloved Rags refuses to go out with him until he promises her a sight of the Prince of Wales, provides her with a brilliant nightclub called Hole in the Sky, an elevator boy posing as the Prince of Wales traveling incognito, and an accusation (leveled at himself) of murder followed by an exciting but foiled attempt at escape from the police. Rags is, of course, won over by this brilliant display: "'Was the whole thing just mine?... Was it a perfectly useless, gorgeous thing, just for me?'"[42]

Some of the stories in *All the Sad Young Men* are interesting, however, because of their use of basic stiuations which Fitzgerald had used before and would use again in *The Great Gatsby*. As Fitzgerald said in 1933:

[40] *Ibid.*, pp. 264–68.

[41] Fitzgerald first used the formula in "The Offshore Pirate," collected in his first volume of short stories, *Flappers and Philosophers* (New York: Charles Scribner's Sons, 1920). Ardita Farnam refuses to meet Toby Moreland, the son of her uncle's rich friend. While she is alone on her uncle's yacht, it is boarded by a negro jazz band with a white "pirate" leader, who has committed some terrible crime and is escaping from the police. The pirate directs the yacht to an unnamed island. Meantime, a romance develops between the criminal and Ardita, and, when the yacht is overtaken, all is discovered: the pirate is none other than Toby Moreland. Ardita is won over: "'What an imagination!' she said softly and almost enviously. 'I want you to lie to me just as sweetly as you know how for the rest of my life.'"

[42] F. Scott Fitzgerald, *All the Sad Young Men* (New York: Charles Scribner's Sons, 1926), p. 158.

> Mostly, we authors must repeat ourselves – that's the truth. We have two or three great and moving experiences in our lives – experiences so great and moving that it doesn't seem at the time that anyone else has been so caught up and pounded and dazzled and astonished and beaten and broken and rescued and illuminated and rewarded and humbled in just that way ever before.
>
> Then we learn our trade, well or less well, and we tell our two or three stories – each time in a new disguise – maybe ten times, maybe a hundred, as long as people will listen.[43]

Fitzgerald could still write with strong feeling in 1936 about the "moving experience" out of which he derived many of his stories:

> It was one of those tragic loves doomed for lack of money, and one day the girl closed it out on the basis of common sense. During a long summer of despair I wrote a novel instead of letters, so it came out all right, but it came out all right for a different person. The man with the jingle of money in his pocket who married the girl a year later would always cherish an abiding distrust, an animosity, toward the leisure class – not the conviction of a revolutionist but the smouldering hatred of a peasant. In the years since then I have never been able to stop wondering where my friends' money came from, not to stop thinking that at one time a sort of *droit de seigneur* might have been exercised to give one of them my girl.[44]

This excruciatingly painful experience provided Fitzgerald with material for the Rosalind-Amory episode in *This Side of Paradise*, for two short stories in *All the Sad Young Men* ("Winter Dreams" and "'The Sensible Thing.'"), and for *The Great Gatsby*.

"Winter Dreams" appears to be an early and much shortened version of *The Great Gatsby*. A contrast of the novel and short story demonstrates the vastly different achievements resulting from the use of different techniques to develop an identical theme. At the center of "Winter Dreams" is Dexter Green's illusion of Judy Jones, an illusion which grows ridiculously out of proportion to its object, just as Gatsby's dream is to begin with Daisy but inflate to an epic vision. The patterns of action of the two stories are similar, varying primarily in material circumstances. The short story opens with Dexter Green, a fourteen-year-old caddy, on the golf course indulging in his winter dreams of wealth and grandeur: "October filled him with hope which November raised to a sort of ecstatic triumph.... He became a golf champion... Stepping from a Pierce-Arrow automobile... surrounded by an ad-

[43] Fitzgerald, "One Hundred False Starts," *op. cit.*, p. 65.
[44] Fitzgerald, "The Crack-Up," *The Crack-Up*, p. 77.

miring crowd, he gave an exhibition of fancy diving from the spring-
board of the club raft." Dexter is suddenly precipitated from his dreams
by the sight of eleven-year-old Judy Jones, who, under the supervision
of her governess, is looking for a caddy. He sees that she is "beautifully
ugly as little girls are apt to be who are destined after a few years to be
inexpressibly lovely and bring no end of misery to a great number of
men." Instead of caddying for the temperamental Miss Jones (at one
point she cries, "'You darn little mean old *thing*!'" to her governess)
as he is ordered to by the caddy-master, Dexter quits his job: "As so
frequently would be the case in the future, Dexter was unconsciously
dictated to by his winter dreams."[45]

Dexter Green appears next at the age of twenty-three, after he has
attended a "famous university in the East, where he was bothered by
his scanty funds," and has started on his way to a fortune in a fancy
laundry business. While playing golf with those for whom he formerly
caddied, he sees again the now mature and "amazingly beautiful" but
still temperamental Judy Jones. There follows a fast affair, "with kisses
that were not a promise but a fulfillment... Dexter surrendered a part
of himself to the most direct and unprincipled personality with which
he had ever come in contact." But Judy quickly grows bored with
Dexter, and he eventually drifts into an engagement with the much less
exciting and even dull Irene Scheerer. Shortly before the engagement
is to be announced, Judy Jones, now "a slender enamelled doll in cloth
of gold," sweeps into his life again. "Judy's flare for him endured just
one month,"[46] but that was long enough to shatter the engagement with
Irene Scheerer.

The final scene of the story is laid in New York, where Dexter, now
thirty-two, is visited in his office on Wall Street by Devlin, a business
man from Detroit, who, it turns out, knows Judy Jones. Devlin casually informs Dexter that her husband, Lud Simms, "has gone to pieces
in a way.... She's a little too old for him." Dexter is on the verge of
assaulting Devlin for what he considers his derogatory remark about
Judy, but Devlin persists in his assertion that Judy's beauty is swiftly
vanishing:

> Dexter looked closely at Devlin, thinking wildly that there must
> be a reason for this, some insensitivity in the man or some private
> malice.
> "Lots of women fade just like *that*," Devlin snapped his fingers.
> "You must have seen it happen. Perhaps I've forgotten how pretty

[45] Fitzgerald, *All the Sad Young Men*, pp. 58–62.
[46] *Ibid.*, pp. 63–85.

she was at her wedding. I've seen her so much since then, you see. She has nice eyes."

A sort of dullness settled down upon Dexter. For the first time in his life he felt like getting very drunk.... When, in a few minutes, Devlin went he lay down on his lounge and looked out the window at the New York sky-line into which the sun was sinking in dull lovely shades of pink and gold.

Dexter's obsessive remembrance of Judy Jones has created in his mind a legendary and impossible vision, and the vision rests on his assurance of not only the reality but eternity of her beauty. When he is emotionally convinced that she has faded, the vision vanishes: "The dream was gone. Something had been taken from him."[47]

Dexter's story closely parallels the story of Gatsby, with the major exception of the ending: Gatsby's illusion is never destroyed. But since "Winter Dreams" is related in the traditional, conventional manner from the point of view of Dexter, who is obviously incapable of explaining the vast and alluring dream which has him in its possession, Fitzgerald must, of necessity, perform the function which Nick Carraway performs in *The Great Gatsby*: the author must interpret for the reader the import and meaning of Dexter's illusion. In performing this function Fitzgerald seems to lecture the reader on particular elements of the story:

> Now, of course, the quality and the seasonability of these winter dreams varied, but the stuff of them remained.... But do not get the impression, because his winter dreams happened to be concerned at first with musings on the rich, that there was anything merely snobbish in the boy. He wanted not association with glittering things and glittering people – he wanted the glittering things themselves. Often he reached out for the best without knowing why he wanted it – and sometimes he ran up against the mysterious denials and prohibitions in which life indulges. It is with one of those denials and not with his career as a whole that this story deals.[48]

And again:

> He wanted to take Judy Jones with him. No disillusion as to the world in which she had grown up could cure his illusion as to her desirability.
>
> Remember that – for only in the light of it can what he did for her be understood.[49]

[47] *Ibid.*, pp. 87–89.
[48] *Ibid.*, pp. 62–63.
[49] *Ibid.*, p. 77.

By such meditation aloud in the presence of the reader, made necessary because of his choice in point of view, Fitzgerald tends to destroy verisimilitude. It is difficult to believe in Dexter's dream or its magnitude with the author frequently intruding to comment on it. Nick Carraway's speculation and comment on Gatsby's dream, appearing naturally within the framework of *The Great Gatsby*, seem an integral part of the story rather than an interruption of the action.

Moreover, "Winter Dreams" is narrated chronologically, covering a period of some eighteen years: no one scene seems to be granted more significance than any others. Fitzgerald attempts to present graphically the growth of Dexter's dream. The episode in which Dexter first sees Judy, during which the dream is born, is rendered as dramatic scene, as well as the episodes following, which bring Dexter and Judy together. By attempting to present all of these episodes as drama, Fitzgerald increases the difficulty of his task, for the realism of the scenes militates against Dexter's unreal illusion. Dexter's dream would be more convincing, perhaps, if these episodes showing its origin were viewed in retrospect, perhaps by Dexter, not as they *were* but as he *remembered* them. When the reader is informed that Judy Jones is an "unprincipled personality," even though he knows that it is not Dexter's knowledge but the author's, belief in the depth of Dexter's illusion becomes difficult. The chronological narration creates time-gaps which must be filled with a number of transitions, sometimes awkward or crude: "This story is not his [Dexter's] biography, remember, although things creep into it which have nothing to do with those dreams he had when he was young. We are almost done with them and with him now. There is only one more incident to be related here, and it happens seven years farther on."[50] By confessing confidentially to the reader the difficulties of his craft, Fitzgerald seems bent on destroying any opportunity for the creation of suspense building to a convincing climax. The action of *The Great Gatsby* is, in contrast, crowded into one brief summer, with episodes of the past reconstructed when and where necessary with lesser or greater treatment according to the demands of the center of the story — Gatsby's dream. By the use of such a tight structure in his novel, Fitzgerald renders it almost impossible for "things [to] creep into it which have nothing to do" with the theme.

The closing lines of "Winter Dreams" offer an interesting contrast to those of *The Great Gatsby*:

> For he [Dexter] had gone away and he could never go back any
> more. The gates were closed, the sun was gone down, and there

[50] *Ibid.*, p. 86.

was no beauty but the gray beauty of steel that withstands all time. Even the grief he could have borne was left behind in the country of illusion, of youth, of the richness of life, where his winter dreams had flourished.

"Long ago," he said, "long ago, there was something in me, but now that thing is gone. Now that thing is gone, that thing is gone. I cannot cry. I cannot care. That thing will come back no more."[51]

By the power of lyrical, rhythmic language, Fitzgerald seems to be attempting to extend and multiply meaning, to evoke a vision of Dexter's dream which goes far beyond it. But the attempt does not quite come off; Fitzgerald's choices of technical devices throughout his story, and even in the conclusion, prevent Dexter's illusion from becoming much more than his own private affair, a matter of his own sickness of spirit. The "poetry" at the close of the story, at first a part of the "exposition," is at the very end voiced by Dexter. The style contains a basic falseness that renders it unconvincing, improbable, and, in Dexter, incongruous ("that thing" is a particularly inept phrase to receive so much emphasis). In the conclusion of *The Great Gatsby*, Nick Carraway is dramatically placed at night among the ruins of the tragedy he has witnessed; his lyrical meditations on the significance of what he has seen are utterly convincing and evocative of a multitude of meaning.

"'The Sensible Thing'" is a less serious treatment of Fitzgerald's "moving experience," but the pattern is easily recognized: "At present he [George O'Kelly] was an insurance clerk at forty dollars a week with his dream slipping fast behind him. The dark little girl who had made this mess... was waiting to be sent for in a town in Tennessee." But the "dark little girl" has made up her mind that she can't marry the poor boy "because it doesn't seem to be the sensible thing." So the poor boy disappears and shows up a year later, George O'Kelly from Cuzco, Peru: "In this short time he had risen from poverty into a position of unlimited opportunity." The "dark little girl" resists George at first — but then succumbs to his charming wealth:

All the time in the world — his life and hers.
But for an instant as he kissed her he knew that though he search through eternity he could never recapture those lost April hours. He might press her close now till the muscles knotted on his arms — she was something desirable and rare that he had fought for and made his own — but never again an intangible whisper in the dusk, or on the breeze of night....
Well, let it pass, he thought; April is over, April is over. There are all kinds of love in the world, but never the same love twice.[52]

[51] *Ibid.*, p. 90.
[52] *Ibid.*, pp. 218–38.

Even in this debased version, there exists the dream or illusion, and, even though the hero gets the girl, he still suffers a keen sense of loss; the "intangible whisper in the dusk, or on the breeze of night" cannot be recaptured, for it is the irrecoverable past.

"Absolution" is of interest not only because of its intrinsic merit as a short story but also because it was first written as a prologue to *The Great Gatsby*.[53] It achieves something of the compact structure of the novel by its use of a frame: the story opens with an eleven-year-old boy, Rudolph Miller, visiting a priest, Father Schwartz, to confess a "terrible sin" (twice he had told a lie in the confessional). After Rudolph begins to relate his sin in somewhat incoherent language, there is a break in the text and his story is continued in the third person; in the final scene, the boy has just finished telling what he has done and is awaiting the reaction of the priest. The materials for the frame come from a splitting of the final episode of the narrative; the previous events are placed between the two halves. Since the transition in Rudolph, with which the story is primarily concerned, is achieved in this final episode, the frame is an integral part of the story. Such a rearrangement of the chronology does more, however, than give form and unity to the story. The opening scene permits the representation of the priest's thoughts at the opening of the story before Rudolph is introduced: this initial characterization of the man who listens to Rudolph's tale colors all of the following incidents related from Rudolph's point of view and establishes the probability of the confirmation of Rudolph's "own inner convictions."

In "Absolution," Fitzgerald has apparently attempted and perhaps achieved the art of "magic suggestiveness." He has focused attention on Rudolph's visit to the priest, an incident which, because it portrays a crucial change in the boy, suggests much more than is explicitly stated about Rudolph's character and future. After he has finished relating his "terrible sin," Rudolph listens to the priest mutter incoherently of "things going glimmering" and of a glittering fair, which "will just hang out there in the night like a colored balloon – like a big yellow lantern on a pole." Rudolph somehow understands:

> ... underneath his terror he felt that his own inner convictions were confirmed. There was something ineffably gorgeous somewhere that had nothing to do with God. He no longer thought that God was angry at him about the original lie, because He must have understood that Rudolph had done it to make things finer in the confessional, brightening up the dinginess of his admissions by

53 Arthur Mizener, *The Far Side of Paradise*, p. 172.

saying a thing radiant and proud. At the moment when he had affirm-
ed immaculate honor a silver pennon had flapped out into the
breeze somewhere and there had been the crunch of leather and
the shine of silver spurs and a troop of horsemen waiting for a
dawn on a low green hill.[54]

This strange vision, perhaps a child's version of the Gatsby dream,
seems to have developed from a glimmering abstraction into a concrete image, and not far from the surface there seems to be a sensual or
even sexual motivation. The Swede girls, whose laughter at the opening
of the story made Father Schwartz "pray aloud for the twilight to
come," reappear at the end of the story in a brilliant vignette:

> Outside the window the blue sirocco trembled over the wheat,
> and girls with yellow hair walked sensuously along roads that
> bounded the fields, calling innocent, exciting things to the young
> men who were working in the lines between the grain. Legs were
> shaped under starchless gingham, and rims of the necks of dresses
> were warm and damp. For five hours now hot fertile life had burn-
> ed in the afternoon. It would be night in three hours, and all
> along the land there would be these blonde Northern girls and the
> tall young men from the farms lying out beside the wheat, under
> the moon.[55]

This tableau, charged throughout with sexual suggestion, serves as
a backdrop to point up dramatically the incoherent frustrations of the
old Catholic priest, celibate by profession, and the inchoate awakening
of the eleven-year-old boy, just emerging on "the lonely secret road of
adolescence."

Though discarded as a prologue to *The Great Gatsby*, "Absolution"
does serve as a prologue to Fitzgerald's new technique, his art of "magic
suggestiveness." As Carl Van Vechten said in reviewing *The Great
Gatsby*, "When I read Absolution in the *American Mercury* I realized
that there were many potential qualities inherent in Scott Fitzgerald
which hitherto had not been too apparent."[56] These potentialities were
realized magnificently in *The Great Gatsby*.

III. BOATS AGAINST THE CURRENT

Shortly before publication of *The Great Gatsby*, Fitzgerald wrote to
John Peale Bishop, "[one of the] cheerfulest things in my life [is]... the

---

[54] Fitzgerald, *All the Sad Young Men*, pp. 130–31.
[55] *Ibid.*, pp. 109–132.
[56] Van Vechten, "Fitzgerald on the March," *op. cit.*, p. 576.

hope that my book has something extraordinary about it."[57] Although one reviewer thought that *The Great Gatsby* was "a book of the season only,"[58] and another that it was "not a good book, but... superior to his [Fitzgerald's] others with the exception of the first,"[59] most reviewers agreed with Fitzgerald that there was something "extraordinary" about his novel. William Rose Benet's review summarized the extraordinary qualities: "The Great Gatsby reveals thoroughly matured craftsmanship. It has structure. It has high occasions of felicitous, almost magic, phrase. And most of all, it is out of the mirage. For the first time Fitzgerald surveys the Babylonian captivity of this era unblinded by the bright lights."[60] Almost every reviewer, like Benet, noted Fitzgerald's new moral perspective and skilled craftsmanship. Had Fitzgerald not matured in his attitude toward his material, his technique would have failed; had he not developed an "esthetic ideal," his theme would have been obscured. Actually, Fitzgerald achieved so rare a balance among the many demanding requirements of fiction that, as one critic said, *The Great Gatsby* "is an almost perfectly fulfilled intention."[61]

Jay Gatsby is the most clearly projected of the tribe of Fitzgerald heroes who are in pursuit of an elusive dream which, even though sometimes within their grasp, continues somehow to evade them. What makes Gatsby tower over Amory Blaine, Dexter Green, and George O'Kelly is the greater magnitude of his glittering illusion and the singlemindness with which he tries to make it a reality. In *The Great Gatsby*, the disastrous events of the summer of 1922 which bring to a close Gatsby's quest of the "grail" (179)[62] are related by Nick Carraway. He is the witness of a series of bizarre scenes in which Gatsby comes close to the attainment of Daisy Buchanan, who personifies the dazzling world of his vision, but fails when he is caught in the backwash of the tawdry affair between Tom Buchanan and his mistress, Myrtle Wilson. Gatsby, unlike the other Fitzgerald heroes, sacrifices his life on the altar of his dream, unaware that it is composed of the ephemeral stuff of the past.

In *The Great Gatsby*, Fitzgerald abandoned the omniscient point of

---

[57] Fitzgerald, "Letters to Friends," *The Crack-Up*, p. 269.
[58] Paterson, "Up to the Minute," *op. cit.*, p. 6.
[59] "New Books in Brief Review," *The Independent*, CXIV (May 2, 1925), 507.
[60] William Rose Benet, "An Admirable Novel," *The Saturday Review of Literature*, I (May 9, 1925), 740.
[61] Paterson, "Up to the Minute," *op. cit.*, p. 6.
[62] Quotations from *The Great Gatsby* (New York: Charles Scribner's Sons, 1925) will be identified in the text by page numbers in parentheses.

view he had previously used in his novels and resorted to first-person narration, after the manner of Joseph Conrad. Until Conrad's special use of the first person, the method had been in disrepute among writers who thought of fiction primarily in terms of technique. Henry James, as Richard P. Blackmur has said, "bore a little heavily against this most familiar of all narrative methods."[63] James thought that the method led inevitably to irrelevance and saturation. In discussing the representation of Strether in *The Ambassadors*, James remarked, "Suffice it, to be brief, that the first person, in the long piece, is a form foredoomed to looseness, and that looseness, never much my affair, had never been so little so on this particular occasion."[64] Although James's comments on Strether are concerned with the *first person* as hero, his points seem aimed against the method generally. James had plenty of examples from literary history of novels in the first person which were chronicles "foredoomed to looseness." *David Copperfield* is one that comes readily to mind; Willa Cather's *My Ántonia* is a modern example of such a novel with "variety... smuggled in by the back door."

But Conrad's use of the first person did not lead to the looseness which James so much feared. In *The Nigger of the Narcissus* (1897), Conrad began as the omniscient author but, after a few pages, shifted to the first person, placing the narrator on board the ship among the crew. The alternation between the first and third persons continued throughout the novel, and, as Joseph Warren Beach says, "technically it appears as a kind of exercise in story-telling, *in the course of which* only he [Conrad] stumbled upon methods which might come in as a supplement to the nice power of words."[65] Conrad exploited the "modified" first-person technique in a series of stories – "Youth," "Heart of Darkness," *Lord Jim*, and *Chance* – in which Marlow acts as narrator, but not in the conventional first-person manner. By the use of a series of technical devices, Conrad avoided the usual pitfalls and limitations of first-person narration.

In *Chance*, for example, the story is told by Marlow to "me," presumably the author, who appears very little except to ask questions now and then of the narrator. Marlow relates the story in the first person, but, when he finds that he cannot "reconstruct" an event (and he is allowed considerable liberties of imagination), he does not hesitate to quote extensively a character who possesses the particular knowledge

---

[63] Richard P. Blackmur, "Introduction," *The Art of the Novel*: Critical Prefaces, by Henry James (New York: Charles Scribner's Sons, 1947), p. xxix.
[64] James, *The Art of the Novel*, p. 320.
[65] Beach, *The Twentieth Century Novel*, p. 349.

that he desires. A character quoted by Marlow may in turn relay information from another character, so that the happening, by the time it reaches the reader, has in effect filtered through a number of minds. In this way Conrad makes the first person narrative serve him as a flexible device in presenting a variety of points of view. But always there, relentlessly pursuing the "subject," is Marlow, who "hold[s] up unquestioningly... the rescued fragment" to search out "the substance of its truth."

In spite of his dislike for first-person narration because of its inevitable "looseness," Henry James, it will be recalled, cited Conrad's *Chance* as an example of the novel of selection. Conrad, James said, had multiplied "his creators or... producers, as to make them almost more numerous and quite emphatically more material than the creatures and the production itself." By placing the narrator in the story and letting him reconstruct and interpret, by turning over all of his "duties" as author to him, Conrad succeeded in effacing himself almost completely. The reader remains unconscious of the author behind the scenes but he becomes acutely conscious of the narrator as a character in the story.

Fitzgerald used the modified first-person in *The Great Gatsby* much as Conrad used it in the Marlow stories. Nick Carraway is charged with relating the story as he sees it, reconstructing by some means whatever he himself has been unable to witness. His qualification as a sympathetic listener is carefully established on the first page of the novel: "I'm inclined to reserve all judgments, a habit that has opened up many curious natures to me and also made me the victim of not a few veteran bores..." Such a characteristic is mandatory for an observer who must rely to a great extent on other people for information about those events which he himself is unable to witness.

There are three methods by which Nick Carraway informs the reader of what is happening or has happened in *The Great Gatsby*: most frequently he presents his own eye-witness account; often he presents the accounts of other people, sometimes in their words, sometimes in his own; occasionally he reconstructs an event from several sources – the newspapers, servants, his own imagination – but presents his version as connected narrative. Nick is initially placed at the edge of the story: he rents a cottage next to Gatsby's mansion in West Egg, and he is remotely related to the Buchanans (he is "second cousin once removed" to Daisy, and he was at Yale with her husband, Tom), who live across the bay in East Egg. This slight relationship is gradually strengthened, particularly through Jordan Baker, whom he meets at the Buchanans, until Nick becomes, in spite of his reluctance, involved in Gatsby's pursuit of Daisy, the material symbol of his dream." Nick's position becomes such that he is naturally able to witness and report personally a maximum of the "contemporary" action. Various devices are used to keep him on stage when Fitzgerald wishes to represent an event scenically through him. During the showdown scene between Tom and Gatsby, Nick informs the reader: "At this point [after it is apparent that an argument between Tom and Gatsby is developing] Jordan and I tried to go, but Tom and Gatsby insisted with competitive firmness that we remain – as though neither of them had anything to conceal and it would be a privilege to partake vicariously of their emotions." (157) Nick's presence is carefully justified in order to enable him to present an eye-witness account of this important incident.

When Fitzgerald needs to inform the reader of material about which his narrator can have no first hand knowledge, he sometimes permits Nick to listen extensively to an individual who has the information. Jordan Baker, one of the most technically useful characters in the book (like a Henry James *ficelle*, however, she is also granted a dramatic interest in the story[66]), informs Nick of the brief war-time love affair between Daisy and Gatsby which had taken place some five years before. Her eye-witness account begins:

> One October day in nineteen-seventeen –
> (Said Jordan Baker that afternoon, sitting up very straight on a straight chair in the tea-garden at the Plaza Hotel).
> – I was walking along from one place to another, half on the sidewalks and half on the lawns. (89)

By this simple device, a past event is represented fully from a point of view other than the narrator's.

Sometimes Fitzgerald permits his narrator to reconstruct in his own language what he has been told about some event he has not witnessed. Citing Gatsby as his source, Nick informs the reader of Gatsby's days with Dan Cody: "James Gatz – that was really, or at least legally, his name. He had changed it at the age of seventeen and at the specific

---

[66] James, *The Art of the Novel*, p. 324: "To project imaginatively, for my hero, a relation [with a *ficelle*] that has nothing to do with the matter (the matter of my subject) but has everything to do with the manner (the manner of my presentation of the same) and yet to treat it, at close quarters and for fully economic expression's possible sake, as if it were important and essential – to do that sort of thing and yet muddle nothing may easily become, as one goes, a signally attaching proposition..." Fitzgerald, it seems, has met and overcome this "signally attaching proposition" admirably: Jordan Baker, who belongs more to the treatment than to the subject, is yet given a well-defined character and a significant role in the action.

moment that witnessed the beginning of his career – when he saw Dan
Cody's yacht drop anchor over the most insidious flat on Lake Superi-
or." (118) This method permits Nick to intersperse speculation and
interpretation with the action: "The truth was that Jay Gatsby of
West Egg, Long Island, sprang from his Platonic conception of himself.
He was a son of God – a phrase which, if it means anything, means
just that – and he must be about his Father's business, the service of a
vast, vulgar, and meretricious beauty." (118) Had he simply "over-
heard" Gatsby telling the story of his youth, the reader would have
been deprived of Nick's imaginative conception of Gatsby's past.

In order to present as dramatically and connectedly as possible a
scene at which there is no surviving observer, Fitzgerald occasionally
allows the narrator to reconstruct an event rather freely from several
sources, unstated but implied. In such a manner Nick describes the
day on which Wilson tracks down and shoots Gatsby and then kills
himself. Nick begins by saying, "Now I want to go back a little and tell
what happened at the garage after we left there the night before." (187)
There follows a dramatic representation of Wilson's eccentric behav-
iour which Nick could have pieced together only from an account by
Wilson's sole companion, Michaelis, who runs a coffee shop near the
Wilson garage. But when Wilson sets out alone in the early morning
on his mission of death, Nick's source of information becomes the newspapers or testimony at the inquest: "His movements – he was on foot
all the time – were afterward traced to Port Roosevelt and then Gad's
Hill, where he bought a sandwich that he didn't eat, and a cup of
coffee... By half-past two he was in West Egg, where he asked some
one the way to Gatsby's house. So by that time he knew Gatsby's
name." (192–93) Nick shifts next to an account of Gatsby's actions at
about this time: "At two o'clock Gatsby put on his bathing-suit and
left word with the butler that if anyone phoned word was to be brought
to him at the pool." (193) At this point and later in his account, Nick
reconstructs Gatsby's actions from various servants – the butler, the
chauffeur, and the gardener. But once Gatsby is alone, Nick's only
resource is his imagination: "He must have looked up at an unfamiliar
sky through frightening leaves and shivered as he found what a grotesque thing a rose is and how raw the sunlight was upon the scarcely
created grass. A new world, material without being real, where poor
ghosts, breathing dreams like air, drifted fortuitously about... like that
ashen, fantastic figure gliding toward him through the amorphous
trees." (194) This entire series of events is pieced together in proper
order, placed in perspective, and presented by Nick as connected

narrative. Whatever deficiencies in knowledge Nick has are made up for amply by his fertile imagination.

Fitzgerald's use of the modified first-person enables him to avoid "the large false face peering around the corner of a character's head."[67] By giving Nick logical connections with the people he is oberserving, by always making his presence or absence at the events probable, not accidental, and by allowing him several natural sources of information which he may use freely, – Fitzgerald achieves a realism impossible to an "omniscient" author or even to a limited third-person point of view: through Nick Carraway, Fitzgerald places the reader in direct touch with the action, eliminating himself, as author, entirely. What Fitzgerald says of Cecilia, in his notes to *The Last Tycoon*, might well apply to Nick in *The Great Gatsby*: "by making Cecilia, at the moment of her telling the story, an intelligent and observant woman, I shall grant myself the privilege, as Conrad did, of letting her imagine the actions of the characters. Thus, I hope to get the verisimilitude of a first person narrative, combined with a Godlike knowledge of all events that happen to my characters."[68] Fitzgerald could have substituted his own name for Conrad's had he recalled Nick Carraway. *The Great Gatsby* is a minor masterpiece illustrating beautifully Conrad's governing literary intent "to make you *see*."

The manner of the representation of events in *The Great Gatsby*, especially the order in which they are related, seems to follow a pattern derived (in part) also from Conrad. Ford Madox Ford, who collaborated with Conrad on a number of early novels, explained the theory behind the re-ordering of events to create a deliberate "confusion":

> It became very early evident to us that what was the matter with the novel, and the British novel in particular, was that it went straight forward, whereas in your gradual making acquaintanceship with your fellows you never do go straight forward. You meet an English gentleman at your golf club. He is beefy, full of health, the moral of the boy from an English Public School of the finest type. You discover gradually that he is hopelessly neurasthenic, dishonest in matters of small change, but unexpectedly self-sacrificing, a dreadful liar... To get such a man in fiction you could not begin at his beginning and work his life chronologically to the end. You must first get him in with a strong impression, and

[67] Fitzgerald, "Introduction," *The Great Gatsby* ("The Modern Library"; New York: Random House, 1934), p. x.

[68] Fitzgerald, *The Last Tycoon*, (New York: Charles Scribner's Sons, 1941), pp. 139–40.

then work backwards and forwards over his past... That theory at least we gradually evolved.[69]

In real life, the story of an acquaintance comes into focus only after apparently unrelated incidents from different periods of time are gradually pieced together; and, unless the individual makes "a strong impression" in the beginning, there is little incentive for one to go to the trouble of discovering the incidents of his life. A story told in this manner gains not only in verisimilitude, however, but also in suspense: pieces of the protagonist's life can be so arranged and revealed as to create mystery, which is particularly effective if there is a sensitive observer to share the reader's bewilderment.

One of the best examples of Conrad's use of this device occurs in *Lord Jim*. Joseph Warren Beach has plotted graphically Conrad's re-arrangement of the chronology in this novel: "The true chronological order would be:

A,B,C,D,E,F,G,H,I,J,K,L,M,N,O,P,Q,R,S,T,U,V,W,X,Y,Z

The order in the book is, by chapters:

KLMP, WA, E, B, E, E, H, GD, HJ, FE, E, E, F, F, F, FK, I, I, R, I, KL, MN, N, Q, QPO, OP, P, QP, P, P, P, QP, P, P, Q, Q, Q, R,ZV, YX, S, S, S, TY, U, U, U, WXY"[70]

This hopelessly scrambled alphabet shows to just what extent Conrad did depart from the traditional "straight forward" method of the British novel. An undated passage in Fitzgerald's notebooks suggests that he was aware of Conrad's method and its purpose: "Conrad's secret theory examined: He knew that things do transpire about people. Therefore he wrote the truth and transposed it to parallel to give that quality, adding confusion however to his structure. Nevertheless, there is in his scheme a desire to imitate life which is in all the big shots."[71] Although this remark might well have been jotted down some time after 1925, Fitzgerald was probably, consciously or unconsciously, following Conrad's method in *The Great Gatsby*.

Fitzgerald does, certainly, get Gatsby in first with a strong impression. When, at the opening of the novel, Nick goes over to the Buchanans for dinner, all he knows about Gatsby is that a man by that name inhabits the fabulous mansion to the right of his cottage. During the course of the evening, Jordan Baker asks Nick if he knows Gatsby, and Nick feels that this "would do for an introduction" (26) when, later that

---

[69] Ford Madox Ford, *Joseph Conrad: A Personal Remembrance* (Boston: Little, Brown, and Company, 1924), pp. 136–37.

[70] Beach, *The Twentieth-Century Novel*, p. 363.

[71] Fitzgerald, "The Note-Books," *The Crack-Up*, p. 179.

evening after he has returned home, he sees Gatsby standing out on his lawn: "But I didn't call to him, for he gave a sudden intimation that he was content to be alone – he stretched out his arms toward the dark water in a curious way, and, far as I was from him, I could have sworn he was trembling. Involuntarily I glanced seaward – and distinguished nothing except a single green light, minute and far away, that might have been the end of a dock. When I looked once more for Gatsby he had vanished, and I was alone again in the unquiet darkness." (26) After this brief but dramatically impressive first glimpse of Gatsby, Fitzgerald works "backwards and forwards" over his past until the complete portrait finally emerges at the end of the book. Just how much Fitzgerald has rearranged the events of Gatsby's life can be seen by tracing events through the book chronologically; the only glimpse of Gatsby's boyhood is in the last chapter; the account of Gatsby, at the age of seventeen, joining Dan Cody's yacht comes in Chapter VI; the important love affair between Gatsby and Daisy, which took place five years before the action in the book when Gatsby, then in the army, first met Daisy, is related three separate times (Chapters IV, VI, and VIII), but from various points of view and with various degrees of fullness; the account of Gatsby's war experiences and his trip, after discharge, back to Louisville to Daisy's home, is given in Chapter VIII; and Gatsby's entry into his present mysterious occupation through Wolfsheim is presented, briefly, in Chapter IX. The summer of 1922, the last summer of Gatsby's life, acts as a string on to which these varicolored "beads" of his past have been "haphazardly" strung.

A simple diagram of the sequence of events in *The Great Gatsby* is, perhaps, helpful. Allowing X to stand for the straight chronological account of the summer of 1922, and A, B, C, D, and E to represent the significant events of Gatsby's past, the nine chapters of *The Great Gatsby* may be charted: X, X, X, XCX, X, XBXCX, X, XCXDX, XEXAX.

Although Gatsby's life is gradually revealed in the novel as an acquaintance's life would probably emerge in real life, there is an artistic order in the disorder. In Nick's pursuit of the "substance of truth" in Gatsby's story, he passes on the information in the order in which he receives it – with one major exception. After briefly recounting Gatsby's days with Dan Cody, he adds: "He [Gatsby] told me all this very much later, but I've put it down here with the idea of exploding those first wild rumors about his antecedents, which weren't even faintly true. Moreover he told it to me at a time of confusion, when I had reached the point of believing everything and nothing about him. So I take advantage of this short halt, while Gatsby, so to speak, caught his breath, to clear this set of misconceptions away." (122) Dozens of legends have accumulated around Gatsby: that he is a cousin of Kaiser Wilhelm, that he killed a man once, that he was a German spy, that he was an Oxford man, that he was involved in the "underground pipe-line to Canada," (117) and even "that he didn't live in a house at all, but in a boat that looked like a house and was moved secretly up and down the Long Island shore." (117) A desirable amount of bewilder-ment, confusion, mystery, and suspense is created by these wild stories, but it is necessary that they gradually give way to something really as awe inspiring as the myths themselves, Gatsby's enormously vital il-lusion. And to understand that illusion, it is necessary to understand its origins, which go far deeper than the love for Daisy. Just as the first half of the novel is devoted to the inflation of the myth of Gatsby to gigantic proportions to give apparent support to the "colossal vitality of his illusion," (116) so the second half gradually deflates this myth through the revelation of the deepness of the roots of Gatsby's dream in the deprivations of his past. The one instance, mid-point in the novel, of Nick's departure from his method of conveying information as it is revealed to him is the book's "fulcrum": the legends must be cleared away so that there might be room for the truth to emerge.

Fitzgerald once remarked of *The Great Gatsby*, "What I cut out of it both physically and emotionally would make another novel."[72] This confession reveals something of the "selective delicacy" with which he dealt with his material. In *The Great Gatsby*, as in neither of his previous novels, the "subject" is unfailingly and remorselessly pursued from beginning to end; yet, contrary to Wells, this novel gives the impression of being more "like life" than either of the other two. Fitzgerald's sympathetic observer, who is narrating the story in retrospect, provides a natural selection, as does the limiting of the action to one summer. But even within these restrictions, Fitzgerald could have indulged in irrelevance or expansiveness. And as a matter of fact, a number of his literary peers criticized *The Great Gatsby* because of its *slightness*. Edith Wharton wrote:

> "My present quarrel with you is only this: that to make Gatsby really Great, you ought to have given us his early career (not from the cradle – but from his visit to the yacht, if not before) instead of a short resumé of it. That would have situated him, & made his

[72] Fitzgerald, "Introduction," *The Great Gatsby* ("The Modern Library"; New York: Random House, 1934), p. x.

final tragedy a tragedy instead of a 'fait divers' for the morning papers."[73]

Fitzgerald wrote to John Peale Bishop,

> It [Bishop's criticism of *The Great Gatsby*] is about the only criticism that the book has had which has been intelligible, save a letter from Mrs. Wharton... Also you are right about Gatsby being blurred and patchy.[74]

Fitzgerald had, of course, experimented with and discarded a prologue to *The Great Gatsby* ("Absolution") which would have revealed much of Gatsby's origin and boyhood. It is a delicate critical problem to determine just how much of Gatsby's past should have been included in the novel. There seems no doubt that Fitzgerald has selected for representation those events of the past which are keys to Gatsby's character and dream. The blurring of Gatsby, if it is a defect, is also a virtue, in that it renders his fantastic illusion more believable.

One of the most effective devices of selection which Fitzgerald employed, enabling him to create the illusion of comprehensiveness and completeness without an actual excess of detail, is the list of names of those who attended Gatsby's parties that fateful summer. Nick tells the reader:

> Once I wrote down on the empty spaces of a time-table the names of those who came to Gatsby's house that summer. It is an old time-table now, disintegrating at its folds, and headed "This schedule in effect July 5th, 1922." But I can still read the gray names, and they will give you a better impression than my generalities of those who accepted Gatsby's hospitality and paid him the subtle tribute of knowing nothing whatever about him.
>
> From East Egg, then, came the Chester Beckers and the Leeches, and a man named Bunsen, whom I knew at Yale, and Doctor Webster Civit, who was drowned last summer up in Maine. And the Hornbeams and the Willie Voltaires, and a whole clan named Blackbuck, who always gathered in a corner and flipped up their noses like goats at whosoever came near. And the Ismays and the Chrysties (or rather Hubert Auerbach and Mr. Chrystie's wife), and Edgar Beaver, whose hair, they say, turned cotton-white one winter afternoon for no good reason at all. (73–74)

The list continues for some two pages, imaginatively evoking a series of fabulous parties attended by an endless number of people – colorful,

[73] Edith Wharton, one of "Three Letters about 'The Great Gatsby,'" *The Crack-Up*, p. 309.
[74] Fitzgerald, "Letters to Friends," *The Crack-Up*, p. 271.

eccentric, fashionable, ambitious, bored – people, who, although they do not know Gatsby, take advantage of the opportunity to drink his liquor and eat his food. Aside from the intrinsic value as superb satire, the device (compare the enumeration of Gloria's suitors in *The Beautiful and Damned*, pp. 144–45) gives the impression, in a very short space and with a minimum of detail, of a continuous round of parties at Gatsby's place – an impression which prevents from seeming arbitrarily selective the scenic presentation of the two parties concerned directly with the "subject."

The Great Gatsby is constructed as a series of scenes dramatizing the important events of the story and connected by brief passages of interpretation and summary. The first three chapters of the book, for example, are devoted to the preparation for and presentation of three scenes: the comparatively "proper" dinner party at the Buchanan's in East Egg, the wild drunken party at Tom and Myrtle's apartment in New York, and the huge, extravagant party at Gatsby's mansion in West Egg. These scenes serve to introduce, dramatically, all of the important characters and places in the novel and seem, perhaps, so selective as to give the impression of artificiality. As though aware of this possibility, Nick confides to the reader at the end of the third scene:

> Reading over what I have written so far, I see I have given the impression that the events of three nights several weeks apart were all that absorbed me. On the contrary, they were merely casual events in a crowded summer, and, until much later, they absorbed me infinitely less than my personal affairs.
>
> Most of the time I worked. In the early morning the sun threw my shadow westward as I hurried down the white chasms of lower New York to the Probity Trust. (68)

This summary of Nick's more or less routine life, which consumes some three or four pages, gives a realistic touch to the book without weighting it with unnecessary and irrelevant detail. Fitzgerald's sure touch in selecting the relevant events for dramatic representation, and for relegating the only obliquely related incidents to summary treatment or panoramic narration, enables him not only to sustain a compelling verisimilitude but also to avoid the "looseness" which Henry James thought inevitable in first-person narration.

In "The Rich Boy," Fitzgerald suggested the manner in which he had achieved objectivity – the way in which he had kept himself from being blinded by the glittering shimmer of superficial sophistication: "Let me tell you about the very rich. They are different from you and me. They possess and enjoy early, and it does something to them, makes them soft where we are hard, and cynical where we are trustful, in a way that, unless you were born rich, it is very difficult to understand.... They are different. The only way I can describe young Anson Hunter [the protagonist] is to approach him as if he were a foreigner and cling stubbornly to my point of view. If I accept his for a moment I am lost – I have nothing to show but a preposterous movie."[75] Too often in his previous novels and stories, Fitzgerald had been unable to differentiate between his own and the points of view of his fabulous characters, and too often he had ended with nothing but a "preposterous" scenario. In *The Great Gatsby*, as in "The Rich Boy" written immediately after, Fitzgerald clung stubbornly to his point of view, the mature view of a disinterested observer gifted with an acute sense of the "fundamental decencies."

Fitzgerald fulfills the obligation imposed by the device of the sensitive observer of making *The Great Gatsby* in some sense the observer's story by portraying Nick Carraway's gradual penetration to the corruption at the heart of the fabulous life of the rich Tom and Daisy Buchanan, and, simultaneously, his gradual discovery of the fundamental innocence and the measureless vitality of Gatsby's dream. While Nick Carraway is recounting this change, a major modification of his initial judgments, he is guiding the reader to a similar moral evaluation of the characters. In the opening pages of the book, Fitzgerald establishes his narrator's moral position. Nick Carraway is, on the advice of his father, "inclined to reserve all judgments" (1) because he knows that "a sense of the fundamental decencies is parcelled out unequally at birth." (2) But his tolerance has a limit: "Conduct may be founded on the hard rock or the wet marshes, but after a certain point I don't care what it's founded on. When I came back from the East last autumn I felt that I wanted the world to be in uniform and at a sort of moral attention forever; I wanted no more riotous excursions with privileged glimpses into the human heart." (2) With Nick Carraway's attitude precisely established at the opening of the story, there can be no ambiguity, as there had been in Fitzgerald's previous novels, regarding the moral quality of his characters or the moral significance of their actions.

In one sense the moral conflict in the novel is resolved into a conflict between East and West – the ancient and corrupt East and the raw but virtuous West. Nick Carraway attributes his moral attitude to his Middle Western background. At the end of the story, he asserts, "I see now that this has been a story of the West, after all – Tom and Gatsby,

[75] Fitzgerald, *All the Sad Young Men*, pp. 1–2.

Daisy and Jordan and I, were all Westerners, and perhaps we possessed some deficiency in common which made us subtly unadaptable to Eastern life." (212) It is perhaps subtly significant that Tom and Daisy live in *East* Egg, since they are really better adapted to Eastern life than Nick and Gatsby, who live in *West* Egg. Perhaps Fitzgerald in dramatizing the conflict of East and West was remembering Edmund Wilson's advice: "it seems to me a great pity that he [Fitzgerald] has not written more of the west; it is perhaps the only milieu that he thoroughly understands; when he approaches the east, he brings to it the standards of the wealthy west – the preoccupation with display, the love of magnificence and jazz, the vigorous social atmosphere of amiable flappers and youths comparatively unpoisoned as yet by the snobbery of the east."[76] Nick's experience in the East results in his return with relief to the West: "After Gatsby's death the East was haunted for me like that [a night scene by El Greco], distorted beyond my eyes' power of correction. So when the blue smoke of brittle leaves was in the air and the wind blew the wet laundry stiff on the line I decided to come back home." (213) "Back home," it seems clear, is a place where the fundamental decencies are observed and virtue is honored.

Tom and Daisy Buchanan represent the world of sophistication which had heretofore, by the sheer brightness of its glamour, blinded Fitzgerald to its frequent lack of a sense of those "fundamental decencies." Racial prejudice, when mouthed by Maury Noble in *The Beautiful and Damned*, had seemed smart philosophizing, even an important idea; when Tom Buchanan says, "It's up to us, who are the dominant race, to watch out or these other races will have control of things," (16) Nick Carraway sees that "something was making him [Tom] nibble at the edge of stale ideas as if his sturdy physical egotism no longer nourished his peremptory heart." (25) When Gloria (in *The Beautiful and Damned*) had asserted her "fundamental sophistication" by her willingness to sacrifice everyone and everything for her own petty pleasure, she had been admired by the other characters and also, the reader felt, by the author; when Daisy Buchanan exclaims, "Sophisticated – God, I'm sophisticated," Nick Carraway feels the "basic insincerity" (21) of what she says. Upon meeting Tom accidentally after the death of Gatsby, Nick confesses:

> I couldn't forgive him or like him, but I saw that what he had done was, to him, entirely justified. It was all very careless and confused. They were careless people, Tom and Daisy – they smashed up things and creatures and then retreated back into their

[76] Edmund Wilson, "The Literary Spotlight: F. Scott Fitzgerald," *op. cit.*, p. 22.

money or their vast carelessness, or whatever it was that kept them
together, and let other people clean up the mess they had made....
   I shook hands with him; it seemed silly not to, for I felt suddenly
as though I were talking to a child. Then he went into the jewelry
store to buy a pearl necklace – or perhaps only a pair of cuff
buttons – rid of my provincial squeamishness forever. (216)

Daisy and Tom, in spite of the bright gleam of their wealth and the
immensely bored sophistication of their careless lives, are seen for what
they are – as the "foul dust that floated in the wake" (3) of Gatsby's
dreams.

It was only by struggling his way through to an objective view of his
material that Fitzgerald was enabled to develop his theme as lucidly
and emphatically as he did. In *This Side of Paradise*, Rosalind's glamour
had blinded both Amory and the author. In "Winter Dreams," Dexter
Green's illusion had failed to become more than his own private possession. In "'The Sensible Thing,'" George O'Kelly's sense of loss had
seemed no more than the nostalgic remembrance of puppy-love. But in
The Great Gatsby, Fitzgerald for the first time embodied his experience
in a story which is not only realistically convincing but also invested
with a meaning beyond the literal. One reviewer defined the theme
of *The Great Gatsby* as that "of a soiled or rather cheap personality
transfigured and rendered pathetically appealing through the possession
of a passionate idealism."[77] Another reviewer described the book as "a
superb impressionistic painting, vivid in colour, and sparkling with
meaning."[78] Almost as vague as the previous definition is specific, these
remarks do no more than hint at what the novel is about.

Shortly after publication of *The Great Gatsby*, Fitzgerald wrote to
Edmund Wilson, "of all the reviews [of *The Great Gatsby*], even the most
enthusiastic, not one had the slightest idea what the book was about."[79]
The meaning of the novel is, presumably, neither obvious nor to be
comprehended in a simple statement. In one sense, certainly, the theme
is the potential tragedy of passionately idealizing an unworthy and
even sinister object. But this narrow definition does not suggest the
subtlety and complexity of meaning brilliantly achieved by the symbolism, by the imagery, and by the language itself; and it is in these
elements that the book is "sparkling with meaning." This phrase recalls
Conrad's "magic suggestiveness," and it seems likely that Fitzgerald
was attempting to accomplish with language what Conrad had outlin-

[77] Van Vechten, "Fitzgerald on the March," *op. cit.*, p. 576.
[78] George Seldes, "Spring Flight," *The Dial*, LXXIX (August, 1925), 164.
[79] Fitzgerald, "Letters to Friends," *The Crack-Up*, p. 270.

ed in his preface to *The Nigger of the Narcissus:* "And it is only through complete, unswerving devotion to the perfect blending of form and substance; it is only through an unremitting never-discouraged care for the shape and ring of sentences that an approach can be made to plasticity, to colour, and that the light of magic suggestiveness may be brought to play for an evanescent instant over the commonplace surface of words: of the old, old words, worn thin, defaced by ages of careless usage."[80] Fitzgerald has not only confessed that he had the words of Conrad's preface fresh in his mind when he set about to write *The Great Gatsby* but he implied an understanding of Conrad's special use of language to define themes when, in May, 1923, he began a book review with a quotation from Conrad's "Youth": "I did not know how good a man I was till then.... I remember my youth and the feeling that will never come back any more – the feeling that I could last forever, outlast the sea, the earth, and all men... the triumphant conviction of strength, the beat of life in the handful of dust, the glow in the heart that with every year grows dim, grows cold, grows small, and expires too soon – before life itself."[81] Fitzgerald commented on the poetically rhythmical style of "Youth," "since that story I have found in nothing else even the echo of that lift and ring." This phrase, close to Conrad's own "shape and ring," suggests that Fitzgerald was fully aware of Conrad's theory of the use of language to extend meaning, and, moreover, that he was probably attempting to follow in his own work Conrad's high, austere principles.

The closing lines of *The Great Gatsby* do echo the "lift and ring" of the passage Fitzgerald quoted from "Youth," and show how well Fitzgerald had mastered Conrad's art of magic suggestiveness:

> Most of the big shore places were closed now and there were hardly any lights except the shadowy, moving glow of a ferryboat across the Sound. And as the moon rose higher the inessential houses began to melt away until gradually I became aware of the old island here that flowered once for Dutch sailors' eyes – as fresh, green breast of the new world. Its vanished trees, the trees that had made way for Gatsby's house, had once pandered in whispers to the last and greatest of all human dreams; for a transitory enchanted moment man must have held his breath in the presence of this continent, compelled into an aesthetic contemplation he neither understood nor desired, face to face for the last time in history with something commensurate to his capacity for wonder.
> And as I sat there brooding on the old, unknown world, I

[80] Conrad, *The Nigger of the Narcissus,* p. xiii.
[81] Fitzgerald, "Under Fire," *op. cit.,* p. 715.

thought of Gatsby's wonder when he first picked out the green light at the end of Daisy's dock. He had come a long way to this blue lawn, and his dream must have seemed so close that he could hardly fail to grasp it. He did not know that it was already behind him, somewhere back in that vast obscurity beyond the city, where the dark fields of the republic rolled on under the night.

Gatsby believed in the green light, the orgastic future that year by year recedes before us. It eluded us then, but that's no matter – to-morrow we will run faster, stretch out our arms farther.... And one fine morning –

So we beat on, boats against the current, borne back ceaselessly into the past. (217–18)

This passage – a "perfect blending of form and substance" – becomes more and more rhythmical simultaneously with the gradual expansion of the significance of Gatsby's dream. There is first the identification of his dream with the dream of those who discovered and settled the American continent – the "last and greatest of all human dreams"; there is next the association of Gatsby's dream with the dream of modern America, lost somewhere in the "vast obscurity" of the "dark fields of the republic"; finally there is the poignant realization that all of these dreams are one and inseparable and forever without our grasp, not because of a failure of will or effort but rather because the dream is in reality a vision of the receding and irrecoverable past. Nick Carraway's discovery is close to Marlow's knowledge in "Youth" – they both sense "a feeling that will never come back any more," they both watch with an acute sense of tragedy "the glow in the heart" grow dim. At the end of *My Ántonia* Jim Burden could assert that he and Ántonia "possessed" the "precious, the incommunicable past"; the very fact that he felt the compulsion to commit that past to a written record suggests that he felt insecure in its possession. It was Nick's discovery that the past cannot be "possessed"; he had watched Gatsby searching for a past (a "past" that had not even had a momentary existence, that was the invention of his imagination) and, ultimately, finding death in its stead.

The green light at the end of Buchanan's dock will draw us on forever – but we shall never possess our Daisy, for she is a vision that really doesn't exist. Nick Carraway sees the green light when he catches his first brief glimpse of his neighbor; he sees Gatsby standing on his lawn, stretching his arms toward the dark water that separates East Egg from West Egg – Daisy from himself. When Nick looks out across the water there is nothing visible "except a single green light, minute and far away, that might have been the end of a dock." (26) The green

light, the contemporary signal which peremptorily summons the travel-
ler on his way, serves well as the symbol for man in hurried pursuit of
a beckoning but ever-elusive dream. And, if Gatsby's dream has particular application to America, as Lionel Trilling has suggested, probably no better symbol than the green light could be used for America's
restless, reckless pursuit of the "American Dream."[82]

There is one set of symbols which pervades the entire book and which
makes it, perhaps, a sharper commentary on contemporary civilization
than the simple story would at first seem. The symbols exist materially
in a "certain desolate area of land" between West Egg and New York,
near the Wilson garage:

> This is a valley of ashes – a fantastic farm where ashes grow like
> wheat into ridges and hills and grotesque gardens; where ashes
> take the forms of houses and chimneys and rising smoke and, finally,
> with a transcendent effort, of ash-gray men, who move dimly and
> already crumbling through the powdery air. Occasionally a line
> of gray cars crawls along an invisible track, gives out a ghastly
> creak, and comes to rest, and immediately the ash-gray men swarm
> up with leaden spades and stir up an impenetrable cloud, which
> screens their obscure operations from your sight.
> But above the gray land and the spasms of bleak dust which
> drift endlessly over it, you perceive, after a moment, the eyes of
> Doctor T. J. Eckleburg. The eyes of Doctor T. J. Eckleburg are
> blue and gigantic – their retinas are one yard high. They look out
> of no face, but, instead, from a pair of enormous yellow spectacles
> which pass over a non-existent nose. Evidently some wild wag of
> an oculist set them there to fatten his practice in the borough of
> Queens, and then sank down himself into eternal blindness, or
> forgot them and moved away. But his eyes, dimmed a little by
> many paintless days, under sun and rain, brood on over the solemn
> dumping ground. (27–28)

On one level, certainly, the valley of ashes represents the gray, dismal
environment of the Wilsons, and the life of the class to which they
belong. Standing at the edge of the Wilson property, the valley casts its
white ashen dust over them and over all of those who stop at the garage.
But, as Fitzgerald returns to the valley of ashes again and again, and,
as he draws his characters one by one along the highway by its "spasms
of bleak dust," the desolate area begins to take on a greater significance: it becomes the primary backdrop against which the tragedy is
played out. At one point, Fitzgerald refers to the valley as "the waste
land," (29) suggesting that it stands as a symbol for the spiritual aridity

[82] Lionel Trilling, "Introduction," *The Great Gatsby* (New York: James Laughlin
for New Directions 1945), p. viii.

of the civilization about which he writes – the kind of barren and water-less land T. S. Eliot had conceived in his poem of that name.

The gigantic eyes of Doctor T. J. Eckleburg, which "brood on over the solemn dumping ground," also take on greater meaning along with the valley of ashes. When Wilson, after his wife's death, informs Michaelis of his earlier suspicions of her, he gazes out the window:

> Wilson's glazed eyes turned out to the ash heaps, where small gray clouds took on fantastic shapes and scurried here and there in the faint dawn wind.
> "I spoke to her," he muttered, after a long silence. "I told her she might fool me but she couldn't fool God. I took her to the window" – with an effort he got up and walked to the rear window and leaned with his face pressed against it – "and I said 'God knows what you've been doing, everything you've been doing. You may fool me, but you can't fool God!'"
> Standing behind him, Michaelis saw with a shock that he was looking at the eyes of Doctor T. J. Eckleburg, which had just emerged, pale and enormous, from the dissolving night.
> "God sees everything," repeated Wilson.
> "That's an advertisement," Michaelis assured him. Something made him turn away from the window and look back into the room. But Wilson stood there a long time, his face close to the window pane, nodding into the twilight. (191–92)

Just as Wilson comes half-consciously to identify the eyes of Doctor T. J. Eckleburg with God, so the reader gradually becomes aware of them as representative of some kind of detached intellect, brooding gloomily over life in the bleak waste land surrounding it, and presiding fatalistically over the little tragedy enacted as in sacrifice before it.

It is probably because these and other symbols "suggest" rather than "mean" that *The Great Gatsby* survives many readings, and that with each reading it continues to "sparkle with meaning." The charming but sinister world of sophistication represented by Daisy and Tom, the world of illusion and dreams represented by Gatsby, and the world of bleakness and ashen dust represented by the Wilsons, converge and collide catastrophically to create not only a fascinating tale but also a fable filled with "magic suggestiveness." When in 1934, Fitzgerald re-read *The Great Gatsby*, he did not feel "guilty of any discrepancy from the truth... truth or rather the equivalent of the truth, the attempt at honesty of imagination."[83] It is because of Fitzgerald's imaginative adherence to the truth, or its equivalent, in *The Great Gatsby* that the book,

[83] F. Scott Fitzgerald, "Introduction," *The Great Gatsby* ("The Modern Library"; New York: Random House, 1934), p. x.

so much a book of its era, detaches itself from its period to have meaning and significance for a later day.

IV. WITHOUT THIS – NOTHING

· *This Side of Paradise*, in spite of its saturation and its lack of direction,
will retain some measure of interest in literary history because of its
more or less accidental historical position; in 1920 it announced the
advent of the lost generation and signaled the beginning of a decade of
wild revolt of American youth. *The Beautiful and Damned*, although it
·suffers from its sympathetic treatment of shabby, pseudo-sophisticated
ideas, is a better technical performance than *This Side of Paradise* and
will continue to interest, perhaps, because of its portrayal of the wild,
irresponsible youth of the Twenties. *The Great Gatsby* alone of Fitzgerald's first three novels may survive on intrinsic merit alone. Fitzgerald
made the difficult transition from formlessness to form, from *saturation*
to *selection*, in the short period of five years; beginning first with Wells
and Mackenzie, and then passing briefly to Mencken, Fitzgerald finally
found in Joyce, Cather, and particularly in Conrad, the kind of artistic
intent to which he could dedicate his craft. And *The Great Gatsby*, the
superb fulfillment of a mature artistic purpose, stands out in sharp
relief from Fitzgerald's previous work: it is of the period, certainly, like
the other two novels, but it is detached from the period, too, by a
brilliant technique.

In an article called "How to Waste Material," published in May,
1926, Fitzgerald surveyed the contemporary literary scene in America
and found it wanting: "These past seven years have seen the same sort
of literary gold rush [as that of the Nineties]; and for all our boasted
sincerity and sophistication, the material is being turned out raw and
undigested in much the same way." The movement of the "Younger
Generation," of which he had been a part and, in no small sense, the
originator, no longer seemed as significant or vital as it once did: "Some
of the late brilliant boys are on lecture tours (a circular informs me
that most of them are to speak upon the literary revolution!), some
are writing pot boilers, a few have definitely abandoned the literary
life – they were never sufficiently aware that material, however closely
observed, is as elusive as the moment in which it has its existence unless
it is purified by an incorruptible style and by the catharsis of a passionate emotion."[84] Fitzgerald was perhaps remembering the "raw and ·
undigested" material of his early work, in the midst of his elation at

[84] Fitzgerald, "How to Waste Material," *op. cit.*, pp. 262–64.

the critical acclaim that *The Great Gatsby* had just won. Certainly his own career would offer the best example of the necessity of a keen critical awareness in the assimilation of material. He had learned that there was a large gap between "material" and the "realization of material" which only strict considerations of art could fill. There was plenty of "sincerity and sophistication" (of a sort) in *This Side of Paradise*, but it was only through an "incorruptible style" and the "catharsis of a passionate emotion" that Fitzgerald fully realized his material in *The Great Gatsby*.

Shortly before his death in December, 1940, Fitzgerald wistfully surveyed his career: "What little I've accomplished has been by the most laborious and uphill work, and I wish now I'd *never* relaxed or looked back – but said at the end of *The Great Gatsby*: I've found my line – from now on this comes first. This is my immediate duty – without this I am nothing."[85] By the time he wrote *The Great Gatsby*, Fitzgerald had found, in large measure, his "aesthetic ideal" in Conrad, and when he was writing his last novel, he was (as his notes to *The Last Tycoon* indicate) still thinking of his craft in Conradian terms. After *The Great Gatsby* there were no great shifts as there had been before in Fitzgerald's fictional technique; but he did not in his later work continue to achieve the brilliance of his third novel. As he himself realized there was a *relaxation*, a *looking back*, which he came to regret near the end of his brief life; any study of his development after *The Great Gatsby* would have to take into account these personal factors, especially as Fitzgerald revealed and analyzed them in 1936 in "The Crack-Up."

Published in *Esquire* in 1936, these confessions of a spiritual bankrupt are both fascinating and embarrassing – fascinating because Fitzgerald spares no detail in publicly analyzing his moral malaise, embarrassing because he is obviously still keenly involved in a losing emotional struggle to become cured. It is typical that in this painful self-revelation Fitzgerald does not envision himself in heroic terms but rather, in domestic metaphor, as simply a cracked plate – a plate that can "never again be warmed in the stove nor shuffled with the other plates in the dishpan" but which "will do to hold crackers late at night or to go into the ice box under left-overs." Fitzgerald's discovery, which he exposes in public penance, is that he has been "mortgaging" himself "physically and spiritually up to the hilt." He has been living on borrowed energy and feeling. Where the spirit should have been most intimately engaged there has been only sham; Fitzgerald confesses a terrible insight: "I saw that for a long time I had not liked people and things,

---

[85] Fitzgerald, "Letters to Frances Scott Fitzgerald," *The Crack-Up*, p. 294.

but only followed the rickety old pretense of liking."[86] In these "crack-up" pieces one becomes gradually aware that Fitzgerald is not referring to a brief period of only two or even five years, but to the span of his whole career. The moral sickness was always there and in 1936 erupts like an ugly boil for all to see; although painful, perhaps the discharge will aid the cure – or at least relieve the inflammation. Like Melville's Bartleby the scrivener, Fitzgerald seems ready to face the blank wall and stare in profound silence for the remainder of his life, for he seems to have withdrawn completely from the human scene and to have even lost a sense of his own identity – "It was strange to have no self – to be like a little boy left alone in a big house, who knew that now he could do anything he wanted to do, but found that there was nothing that he wanted to do." The only element throughout these terrible revelations which suggests that Fitzgerald is not doomed by self-revulsion is his acute sense of time. At one point he says parenthetically – "I have the sense of lecturing now, looking at a watch on the desk before me and seeing how many more minutes."[87] And later – "The watch is past the hour and I have barely reached my thesis." Only a man who was bent on achievement could possess such an obsessive awareness of time.

The spiritual dilemma described so painfully in "The Crack-Up" goes far toward explaining the ten-year lapse between *The Great Gatsby* and Fitzgerald's fourth novel, *Tender Is The Night.* An account of the many versions through which this novel passed is a story in itself, the last event of which occurred recently with the publication of a "final" version which Fitzgerald had prepared but which he was unable to see through the press. An early version of the novel was to be the story of a man who kills his demanding and dominating mother; subsequent versions shifted focus to what had at first been minor characters. Finally Fitzgerald published the book in 1934, but even publication did not stop him from further tampering with the text. After his death there was discovered among his papers a revised and rearranged copy of *Tender Is The Night* bearing the legend: "This is the *final version* of the book as I would like it." This copy, differing considerably from the published book, was edited and issued in 1951.[88]

Tender Is The Night relates the decline and disintegration of its hero, Dick Diver, from a position of great promise in clinical psychology to the level of a pitifully inept practitioner, moving from town to town in

[86] Fitzgerald, *The Crack-Up*, pp. 72–75.

[87] *Ibid.*, pp. 78–79.

[88] Malcolm Cowley, "Introduction," *Tender Is the Night* (New York: Charles Scribner's Sons, 1951), pp. iii–xii. For a portion of one of the early versions of *Tender*, see, "The World's Fair," *The Kenyon Review*, X (Autumn, 1948), 565–78.

search of his lost self. The causes for the decline are both complex and obscure. Dick Diver has all of the weaknesses of Anthony Patch of *The Beautiful and Damned* together with some of the capacity of vision (but not the illusion) of Jay Gatsby. But Diver's fall from imminence does not somehow constitute the tragedy it was meant to be, probably because of a failure in Fitzgerald's conception. So much of the older versions of the book remains as to render the development of character complex, but the complexity never gives way, as it should, to the lucidity the reader desires. Fitzgerald's technique was adapted to the variety and difficulty of his material. The strictness with which Fitzgerald adheres to the point of view of Rosemary Hoyt in the first one-fourth of the novel seems modeled on the later Henry James of *The Ambassadors*. Eighteen-year-old Rosemary, already a famous movie star, is precisely the person to invest the Riviera scenes she witnesses with the glamour and excitement of her own fresh innocence. The extent to which Fitzgerald brooded over the order of the relation of the events of his story is suggested by a passage in his notebooks:

> Analysis of Tender:
> I Case History 151–212: 61 pp.
> II Rosemary's Angle 3–104: 101 pp.
> III Casualties 104–148, 212-224: 55 pp.
> IV Escape 225–306: 82 pp.
> V The Way Home 306–408: 103 pp.[89]

Fitzgerald has simply rearranged chronologically the series of events he had, in Conradian fashion, disarranged for artistic purposes. In the "re-ordering" of the events in the book, Dick Diver, like Gatsby and Lord Jim, is "gotten in " with a "strong impression" by his introduction through the youthful but sophisticated consciousness of Rosemary. Fitzgerald muddied the already dark waters when he indicated that he wanted his novel reprinted with the events in chronological order, and the last edition of the novel has followed his wishes. Whether because of a shifting conception indicated by the long period of uncertainty and revision, or because of a lack of a motivating or central idea, or, even, because of an inability to handle or subject to unity material of such complexity, Fitzgerald did not achieve in *Tender Is the Night* the structural or technical perfection of *The Great Gatsby*.

Taps at Reveille, Fitzgerald's final volume of short stories, appeared in 1935. Like the three earlier collections, it is uneven in quality, with some of Fitzgerald's best work alongside some of his most mediocre.

[89] Fitzgerald, "The Notebooks," *The Crack-Up*, pp. 180–81.

Of particular interest are the "Basil" and "Josephine" stories, in which Fitzgerald uses material that he has exploited before, particularly in the first part of *This Side of Paradise*. But it is from a vastly different perspective that Fitzgerald now sees his Middle Western boyhood. · Amory Blaine came from a background of wealth and social importance, while Basil Duke Lee knows that he is "one of the poorest boys in a rich boys' school."[90] Rosalind was the ultimate in sophistication, while Josephine, so the author informs us, has "the first mature thought that she had ever had in her life"[91] on the next to last page of her history. If Fitzgerald saw his material more objectively, he also saw it less brilliantly; there is not in these stories the sparkle and life of the first novel. At least two stories of high merit deserve particular mention: "Crazy Sunday," a story of Hollywood which, in some ways, foreshadows the last novel; and "Babylon Revisited," the nostalgic story of a man who returns, after the Depression, to the Left Bank, in an attempt to pick up the pieces of a disintegrated life, but who discovers that he has "lost everything... he wanted in the boom."[92]

In spite of all of his physical and spiritual difficulties, Fitzgerald ambitiously began *The Last Tycoon* in Hollywood, where he spent the greater part of his last years writing for the motion pictures. There is a kind of heroic determination in his letters to his daughter during this period: "Anyhow I am alive again – getting by that October did something – with all its strains and necessities and humiliations and struggles. I don't drink. I am not a great man but sometimes I think the impersonal and objective quality of my talent and the sacrifices of it, in pieces, to preserve its essential value has some sort of epic grandeur."[93] On November 25, 1940, Fitzgerald wrote to Edmund Wilson: "I think my novel [*The Last Tycoon*] is good. I've written it with difficulty. It is completely upstream in mood and will get a certain amount of abuse but it is first hand and I am trying a little harder than I ever have to be exact and honest emotionally.... This sounds like a bitter letter – I'd rewrite it except for a horrible paucity of time. Not even time to be bitter."[94] Fitzgerald's acute consciousness of the swift passage of time now seems like a prophetic awareness of approaching death. He died in December, 1940, without completing his novel, but it was published posthumously with his notes and plans in 1941.

In September, 1940, Fitzgerald wrote to a friend: "But it [*The Last*

[90] Fitzgerald, *Taps at Reveille* (New York: Charles Scribner's Sons. 1935), p. 32
[91] *Ibid.*, p. 199.
[92] *Ibid.*, p. 406.
[93] Fitzgerald, "Letters to Frances Scott Fitzgerald," *The Crack-Up*, p. 291.
[94] Fitzgerald, "Letters to Friends," *The Crack-Up*, p. 285.

Tycoon] is as detached from me as *Gatsby* was, in intent anyhow."[95] In another letter, in which he outlined the story for Scribner's Maxwell Perkins, Fitzgerald said, "If one book could ever be 'like' another, I - should say it is more 'like' *The Great Gatsby* than any other of my books."[96] It is impossible to know whether *The Last Tycoon*, in its rough, unfinished state, would have achieved or surpassed the brilliance of *The Great Gatsby*. But Edmund Wilson, editor of *The Last Tycoon*, has pointed out the chief value of Fitzgerald's last novel: "This draft of *The Last Tycoon*... represents that point in the artist's work where he has assembled and organized his material and acquired a firm grasp of his theme, but he has not yet brought it finally into focus."[97] The incomplete version of the novel together with the notes make a fascinating study for the student of fictional technique. For example, Fitzgerald explains his choice of point of view (the story is told, like *The Great Gatsby*, in the first person by an observer):

> Cecilia is the narrator because I think I know exactly how such a person would react to my story. She is *of* the movies but not *in* them. She probably was born the day *The Birth of a Nation* was previewed and Rudolf Valentino came to her fifth birthday party. So she is, all at once, intelligent, cynical, but understanding and kindly toward the people, great or small, who are of Hollywood.
> She focuses our attention upon two principal characters – Milton Stahr and Thalia, the girl he loves.[98]

In such notes as this, the reader can study the artist's mind in the midst of the job of creation. A fellow artist, John Dos Passos, was not modest in his estimate of the worth of Fitzgerald's final novel: "I have an idea that it will turn out to be one of those literary fragments that from time to time appear in the stream of a culture and profoundly influence the course of future events."[99] Although this estimate is probably exaggerated, it does seem likely that the serious student of the novel will find both the multi-version *Tender* and the fragmentary *Tycoon* excellent sources for the study of fictional technique.

In 1937 Fitzgerald and Thomas Wolfe engaged in an exchange of letters which parallels, in part, the correspondence between Henry James and H. G. Wells of an earlier period. Although Fitzgerald's letter is not available, it is apparent that he took the part of James in urging "selection" as a principle of fiction; Wolfe's reply reveals that

[95] *Ibid.*, p. 282.
[96] Fitzgerald, *The Last Tycoon*, p. 141.
[97] *Ibid.*, p. ix.
[98] *Ibid.*, pp. 138–39.
[99] Dos Passos, "A Note on Fitzgerald," *The Crack-Up*, p. 339.

he accepted the role of Wells: "I suppose I would agree with you in what you say about 'the novel of selected incident' so far as it means anything. I say so far as it means anything because every novel, of course, is a novel of selected incident. There are no novels of unselected incident. You couldn't write about the inside of a telephone booth without selecting. You could fill a novel of a thousand pages with a description of a single room and yet your incidents would be selected."[100] Wolfe insisted on misunderstanding Fitzgerald, just as Wells had misunderstood James; but Wolfe rescues for us Fitzgerald's phrase, "the novel of selected incident," which seems particularly apt for describing *The Great Gatsby;* and its meaning can be readily comprehended by placing Fitzgerald's finely wrought, perfectly shaped novel against the great, amorphous mass which is any one of Thomas Wolfe's novels. It seems appropriate that Fitzgerald should play the part of James in suggesting "selection" to Thomas Wolfe, for it does not seem too much to say, as T. S. Eliot did say, that *The Great Gatsby* was the first step that American fiction had taken since Henry James.

[100] Thomas Wolfe, "A Letter from Thomas Wolfe," *The Crack-Up*, p. 314.

CONCLUSION

If F. Scott Fitzgerald's novels might serve to illustrate the tendencies in fiction toward *saturation* on the one hand and toward *selection* on the other, his development as a writer might serve as the prototype in the "evolution" of fictional technique. From *This Side of Paradise* in 1920 to *The Great Gatsby* in 1925, Fitzgerald's growth in awareness of the artistic possibilities in the writing of fiction is a reflection in miniature of the historical development of such an awareness involving numerous writers over a long period of time. One is tempted to see in the relationship of the development of Fitzgerald as an artist to the development of fiction as an art form a parallel to the biological theory – ontogeny recapitulates phylogeny, or the life cycle of the individual organism reflects the evolutionary cycle of the species. No doubt many writers have followed the pattern of Fitzgerald's development, but seldom has the detail of the pattern emerged so clearly in so concentrated a period.

In a brief recapitulation of Fitzgerald's development, it is perhaps profitable to introduce a metaphor brilliantly elaborated by Henry James in his preface to *The Portrait of a Lady*: "The house of fiction has in short not one window, but a million – a number of possible windows not to be reckoned, rather; every one of which has been pierced, or is still pierceable, in its vast front, by the need of the individual vision and by the pressure of the individual will." In an extension of this figure, James points out that the human scene spread out before the window is the subject, while the window frame itself is the artistic form. James thus views form as that element which gives the artist a relatively "disengaged" perspective, as the element which allows him to remove himself from direct involvement in the experience he is representing.

We may readily understand the nature of Fitzgerald's artistic development by recasting it in the terms of James' metaphor. When he wrote *This Side of Paradise*, Fitzgerald had discovered the complexity and variety of the human scene and he set about with great vitality to embody his impressions in his novel. He felt no need to "retreat" to a house of fiction to view his subject from a sobering distance; indeed, he seemed not even aware that such a house existed. His primary concern amidst the abundance of life was to spend his energies "getting all in" that he possibly could.

By the time he wrote *The Beautiful and Damned*, however, Fitzgerald had made delightful discovery of the house of fiction and had begun his exploration of it – an exploration that seemed in progress as the story was written. Perhaps we can imagine this house of fiction as containing not only many windows but also French doors which allow easy and almost unconscious egress to an outside which curiously gives the illusion of being inside. There is a sense of artistic perspective in parts of *The Beautiful and Damned*, but frequently too there is a strong sense of direct and "distorting" involvement: Fitzgerald seems sometimes to believe that a window is framing his view when in actuality nothing at all separates him from his subject.

In *The Great Gatsby* Fitzgerald seems not only to have explored the house of fiction but to be comfortably at home there. When he set about writing his masterpiece, he had achieved that "individual vision" which comes from the steady but penetrating gaze through the frame of the window. For the first time in his career he was able to disengage himself from his subject and treat his material from an artistic and impersonal perspective. Never again was he able to achieve this perspective: the window became dim, the gaze unsteady.

The dominant influences on Fitzgerald, H. G. Wells in *This Side of Paradise*, H. L. Mencken in *The Beautiful and Damned*, and Joseph Conrad in *The Great Gatsby*, were all individuals whose basic characteristics were fixed along the arc of Fitzgerald's development – Wells as a journalistic novelist, Mencken as a critic careless in the discrimination between art and life, and Conrad as a novelist constantly preoccupied with artistic considerations. Fitzgerald's achievement in *The Great Gatsby* was, in the Conradian manner, to intensify the impression of direct experience by "treating" it indirectly, and, in the Jamesian manner, to deepen the feeling of objectivity by maintaining steadily the selective view through the window of the house of fiction.